REVELATION
A Book of Hope

Lawrence Webb

© 2014 Lawrence Webb
All Rights Reserved

Revelation: A Book of Hope
by Lawrence Webb
ISBN: 978-1500874575

Book design by Nathan Golden

Bible passages are usually in italics to make them more readily identifiable. Unless otherwise indicated, Scripture quotations are from the Revised Standard Version of the Bible, copyright © 1946, 1952, and 1971 the Division of Christian Education of the National Council of the Churches of Christ in the United States of America.
Used by permission. All rights reserved.

Additional copies may be ordered through:
Amazon.com
Createspace.com

Other titles by Lawrence Webb:
Hardin-Simmons, Hail to Thee
Once for a Shining Hour: Reflections on Christmas
Christmas Memories, From Seven to Seventy

Acknowledgements

Various individuals and groups have been exposed to my interpretation of Revelation in several settings over the past decade. Their questions, disagreements, and requests for clarification — along with a few "amens" — have been helpful as I gave this book its present shape. But the standard disclaimer prevails here: Final content, for better or worse, is mine alone.

Groups have included the following:
- Adults at First Baptist Church, Anderson, South Carolina, my home church, in a Wednesday night study group
- The Baraca Radio Sunday School Class I teach each Sunday (current Bible lessons at www.andersonfbc.org/baraca)
- Lifelong Learning classes on Revelation I have taught at Anderson University where I hold the recognition and honor as professor emeritus
- Fellow members of a Lifelong Learning writing workshop, taught by Jan Osburn, as they read part of the evolving manuscript and made constructive comments

I have shared my vision of Revelation with several friends whose evaluation I respect. They have read the emerging manuscript and/or heard my lessons:
- The Rev. Dr. Jim Thomason, my pastor at First Baptist, Anderson
- The Rev. Josh Hunt, our associate pastor
- Dr. Richard DeAngelis, an Anderson dermatologist
- The Rev. Amy Dill Bratton, a United Methodist pastor in Anderson
- The Rev. Dr. Bob Burks, emeritus Bible professor at Anderson University
- Attorney Lloyd Culp, one of my nephews, in Houston
- The Rev. Father Mike Marsh, rector, St. Philip's Episcopal Church, Uvalde, Texas
- The late Julian Smith, M. D., a member of the Baraca Class

who took one of my Lifelong Learning Courses on Revelation courses at Anderson University
- Dr. John Lassiter, professor of history, Anderson University
- I owe a particular debt of gratitude to members of a small working group of writers. We dubbed ourselves the Wordsmiths: the Rev. Dr. Brett Chandler Patterson, CPA Jim Rasheed, and one of my former journalism students, Jeff Sartini. Brett, Jim, and Jeff challenged, cajoled, and confronted me at every turn as I strove for clarity, chapter by chapter.
- A loving word is in order for Pansy, my wife of nearly fifty years, a careful reader and my kind and honest critic.

A final word is due Nathan Golden, another of my former Anderson University students, who has planned and carried out the layout and design of most of my books over the past decade, including this one. He has also cast an editor's eye, page by page, as we have worked to bring it to completion.

Contents

Introduction 7

1 — Revelation Chapter 1:
The Revelation of Jesus Christ 15

2 — Revelation Chapters 2-3:
Letters to Seven Churches 23

3 — Revelation Chapters 4-5:
A Vision Before the Vision..33

4 — Revelation Chapters 6-11:
Seven Seals and Seven Trumpets..41

5 — Revelation Chapters 12-13:
The Woman Clad in the Sun,
the Dragon and the Two Beasts..61

6 — Revelation Chapters 14-16:
Two Series of Three Angels, Seven Bowls of Wrath,
and Preparation for Armageddon...87

7 — Revelation Chapters 17-18:
The Fall of Babylon...97

8 — Revelation Chapter 19:
The Battle of Armageddon 107

9 — Revelation Chapter 20:
The Millennium and the Final Judgment............................ 115

10 — Revelation Chapters 21-22:
The Holy City, New Jerusalem... 127

Appendix A — The Rapture.. 141

Appendix B — The Great Tribulation..................................... 146

Introduction

In Amy's adult Sunday school class, the teacher distributed a list of well-known sayings, some from the Bible, some from other sources. "Cleanliness is next to godliness" was on the list, and Amy argued that the saying was in the Bible. The teacher told her this was said by Susanna Wesley, the mother of John and Charles Wesley, the founders of the Methodist denomination.

Amy continued to insist the saying was in the Bible. So the teacher loaned her a concordance, which helps locate words and phrases in the Bible, and asked Amy to find the statement and bring her report to class next Sunday. When she returned, the teacher asked, "Did you find "Cleanliness is next to godliness" in the Bible?"

Amy said, triumphantly, "It's in *my* Bible. I *wrote* it in."

Our Amy has many counterparts who interpret the biblical book of Revelation. They write in concepts not put there by the author. These add-ons or write-ins include the Rapture and the Antichrist. These hot button end-of-the-world topics, the Rapture and the Antichrist, which we will examine in due time in this book, are never mentioned in Revelation. Even so, a study of Revelation must give attention to *eschatology*, the doctrine of last things, because the book builds to the grand climax of Christ's final triumph over Satan, Death, and Hades.

This book you are reading is designed to help you find what is and is not in Revelation and to help you see Revelation as a book offering hope, rather than fear. You may not recognize hope as the dominant theme because much of the book depicts chaos and disaster on earth and in the sky, unearthly creatures and warfare. But hope is what Revelation is about. It offers hope to Christians in the Roman Empire in the first century who are under fire because they worship Jesus Christ instead of the reigning Caesar. You see, the emperor expects people to acknowledge him as a god by burning incense at his altars. It's okay with him if you want to worship other gods, just so you keep him on your list.

The author employs a kind of code language. For example, there's no mention of Rome or of Caesar. Instead of Rome, we read about the ancient city of Babylon. Instead of Caesar, there's a beast with seven heads, ten horns, and ten crowns on the horns. Also, a whore sits on seven hills. Remember, Rome was built on seven hills.

Yet, early signs of hope come in the opening chapter. In verse 5, Jesus Christ is declared *the first-born of the dead, and the ruler of kings on earth.* Then, in verse 16, in figurative descriptions, Jesus has seven stars in his right hand, and there's a sharp, two-edged sword coming out of his mouth. We can forget the stars for the moment, but the sword is highly significant.

Playwrights and novelists will tell you, if a gun or knife shows up in the first chapter of a book or the first act of a play, you expect that weapon to be used before the story ends. That's true here. The writer named John introduces us to that two-edged sword in the first chapter as a foreshadowing of things to come.

That sword is called a *sharp, two-edged sword* — a description also used in another biblical book: the Epistle to the Hebrews 4:12:

For the word of God is living and active, sharper than any two-edged sword, piercing to the division of soul and spirit, of joints and marrow, and discerning the thoughts and intentions of the heart.

In between the two appearances of the sword in Christ's mouth in Revelation, we see chaos, destruction, and massive threats to those early Christians. But, in the midst of all that, hope breaks through at several points before Christ's final triumph:

In chapter 1, Christ stands among seven churches, holding their pastors in His right hand. In chapters 2-3, He writes letters to the churches, admonishing some but encouraging all to remain faithful. In chapters 4-5, in the throne room of heaven Author John has a vision of God as *one seated on the throne* and of Christ as *a Lamb standing as though it had been slain.* In chapters 6-22, a series of visions unfolds, depicting great disasters along with combat between heavenly and hellish forces, until the final revelation of God's new heaven and new earth in which all is beauty and bliss forever. Hope becomes fruition.

A Word About Chapters and Verses

Chapters in this book are based on units of emphasis in the text of Revelation. In this regard, we need to be aware the Bible was not written in chapters and verses. Around A. D. 1227, Stephen Langton, archbishop of Canterbury, made our present-day chapter divisions to aid readers in finding specific passages. The Wycliffe English Bible of 1382 was the first translation to use this pattern. Rabbi Nathan divided the Hebrew text into verses in the mid-fifteenth century, and Robert Estienne made verse divisions in the New Testament in the mid-sixteenth century. Although chapter and verse divisions make it easier to find desired passages, arbitrary chapter divisions sometimes interrupt the flow of thought.

Let's admit it. Revelation is not exactly easy reading, and many people simply avoid reading it at all because they've heard so many weird things about it. Some of those things they've heard really are in the book, but some were written in by Amy's friends.

Other people start reading but don't go far. Little wonder, given the strange creatures and hard to understand descriptions. For example, when we first encounter Jesus in chapter 1, His head and hair are white as wool or snow, His eyes like a flame of fire, His feet like burnished bronze, His voice like the sound of many waters. And there's that sword in His mouth. In chapters 4-5, there are six-winged creatures covered all over with eyes. Then in chapter 6 come unnatural phenomena: a great earthquake, the sun turning black, the moon becoming blood red, and the stars falling to the earth like leaves from a tree. All this is just for starters.

Most casual readers have long since stopped reading. Many who continue reading still struggle to understand. They ask:

What is it all about?
What does it mean?
Is the world as we know it about to end?

Misunderstanding and fear abound regarding the book:
- Random callers to current affairs talk shows insist we are in the end times and Christ will soon come back to rapture believers out of this sinful world.
- Some members of the U. S. Congress in press conferences and sound bites openly declare these are the last days.
- Residents in some towns reject 666 as the prefix in phone numbers because of what they hear about this number in Revelation.
- Popular novels and movies, as well as preachers on radio and television, get people worried or excited about the end times, seemingly due any day now. Much preaching and writing about Revelation reflects unfettered creativity in people who want to believe things which simply are not in the book. More of Amy's kinfolks.

A major source of the misunderstanding about Revelation and the end time is a system of interpretation developed in England in the 1800s by John Nelson Darby and popularized in the United States early in the twentieth century by C. I. Scofield. Scofield published an edition of the King James Bible with footnotes based on Darby. We will look further at Darby-Scofield in this book.

Given the unusual nature of the book and current popular fiction disguised as Bible interpretation, we should not be surprised at these questions and interpretations. But we will discover the seemingly great mysteries are much easier to unlock than they might first appear.

Seven Keys to Unlock the Mysteries of Revelation

The book itself – together with facts from ancient history – provides help for understanding. Because the number seven is used more than forty times in the text as a symbol of fullness or completeness, let us consider seven keys to help us unlock the mysteries of Revelation:

1. The Historical Setting

We don't know exactly when Revelation was written. For that matter, none of the books of the Bible give their dates of writing. But many scholars believe Revelation was written during the reign of the emperor Domitian in the late decades of the first Christian century, when, as we noted earlier, Christians were under pressure to acknowledge Caesar as god. Those who refused to burn incense at altars to the emperor could face punishment, exile, or death. Revelation is directed toward Christians who faced these and other pressures.

2. The Very First Sentence

In this first sentence, John says he has a revelation of *what must soon take place*:

The revelation of Jesus Christ, which God gave him to show to his servants what must soon take place; and he made it known by sending his angel to his servant John . . .

He apparently expects his vision to be fulfilled soon, rather than centuries later, as some interpret the book.

3. A Message of Hope in Times of Persecution

We saw earlier, letters to seven churches in chapters 2 and 3 precede the main vision of the book. These were actual congregations in seven cities in what was then called Asia Minor, part of modern-day Turkey. John writes distinctive messages to each church, with words of comfort or correction as needed. Yet all seven letters point to God's faithfulness and call the churches to remain faithful in the face of heretical teaching, materialism, and severe testing and tribulation. Christ calls each church to hear what God's Spirit is saying, and Christ promises good to those who conquer in His name. Some of the churches are in the throes of great suffering.

4. Christ the Central Figure

From the start, Jesus Christ is presented as the One with power to conquer evil: He stands among the struggling churches in chapter

1; He offers encouragement and challenge to them in chapters 2 and 3; in chapter 5 He is both the mighty Lion of Judah and the Lamb Who Was Slain. This Lamb is the only One in all creation worthy to open the scroll containing the revelation from God beginning in chapters 6. Amid the calamitous events depicted in the visions, Christ ultimately triumphs over the Devil and his henchmen in chapters 19 and 20.

5. Similarity to Other New Testament Books

In the struggle to understand this admittedly strange book, it is crucial for the reader to realize Revelation is like all other New Testament books in one way:

Every New Testament book – including Revelation – was written with a message for people in the first Christian century. So the first step in understanding each book's primary message must be to learn what the book meant to its original readers. No biblical book was written primarily for readers who will live many centuries later. There are lessons for future generations, including our own, but we first must find the message for those original readers.

6. Crucial Difference from Other New Testament Books

On the other hand, with its weird creatures, symbolism, and mysterious numbers, Revelation stands in sharp contrast with all the other New Testament books. Because it is so different, readers may think Revelation is a unique book. But there were numerous writings with similar characteristics in the years before and after the New Testament was formed. This category of writings is known as *apocalyptic*. In fact, the name of this book in Greek, the language of the New Testament, is *Apocalupsis* or *Apocalypse*. The word simply means *revelation*, though we may feel its strange creatures and mysterious numbers obscure rather than reveal.

Several books in the Old Testament, have apocalyptic passages. These include large portions of Daniel and passages from Ezekiel and Zechariah. Other Jewish apocalyptic writings, which did not find acceptance as holy writ, include some of the Dead Sea Scrolls.

Apocalyptic writing typically focuses on a struggle between God and the forces of evil, with God ultimately the victor. Christians who play end-of-time guessing games turn this spiritual battle into a physical battle to be fought in the very near future at Armageddon. In Revelation, the bottom line is that Christ is in control through all the calamities and will finally conquer evil and make all things new.

7. Obvious Symbolism

Revelation overflows with creatures and settings that beg to be interpreted symbolically rather than literally or historically:
- A red dragon with seven heads, ten horns, and seven crowns whose long tail knocks a third of the stars out of the sky (12:3-4); identified as the Devil and Satan (12:9)
- A woman who sprouts wings and flies away from the dragon when he spews a river out of his mouth in the attempt to destroy her and her son (12:14-16)
- A beast much like the red dragon, with seven heads, ten horns, and ten crowns, resembling a leopard, a bear, and a lion (13:1) with the mysterious number 666 (13:18)
- An army of locusts with human faces, tails which sting like scorpions, and an angel from the bottomless pit to rule over them (9:3-11)
- Death and Hades, the realm of the dead, riding on horses (6:7-8)
- Twelve gates of the New Jerusalem, each made of one huge pearl (21:21)
- A harlot seated on many waters or, alternately, on seven mountains (17:1, 9)

Now, you should keep these seven keys handy on a key ring to use from time to time as we begin our journey into the rich, symbolic biblical text that points us to hope in Jesus Christ.

1 – Revelation, Chapter 1: The Revelation of Jesus Christ

True story: A boy in the second grade was a Methodist preacher's son. The boy's mother, like most mothers, wanted her son to stay clean and healthy. One rainy day, he came in for supper, covered in mud. His mother told him to take a bath, warning, as she often did, that he was likely to pick up germs when he played outside in the mud. Because he had heard this so often, he blurted out, "All I ever hear in this house is germs and Jesus."

In the first chapter of Revelation, never mind the germs, but about all we hear will be Jesus.

Writing to seven churches who face various pressures, the author seeks to identify with them, telling them that he is suffering for his faithfulness to Jesus Christ. He gives an elaborate description of Jesus in two sets of seven attributes, climaxing with the symbolic picture of Jesus standing amid the churches, holding their pastors in His hands.

Important Words and Phrases in the Opening Verses

Word meanings change over time. For example, *quarantine* originally meant a forty-day period, but it has come to mean a time of isolation, with no reference to its specific duration. *Naturally* used to refer to the inherent or innate character or *nature* of something, but its current common usage is another way of saying, "Of course." *Enthusiasm* today means excitement or high interest, and maybe we can see a connection with its original meaning of being filled with God: A person filled with God might well express that indwelling with excitement. *Unique* means the only one of its kind, but it has been diluted to suggest "sorta different" instead of distinctly different from everything else. Thus, things are often described as *very unique* or *somewhat unique*.

The First Word

The first word in the Greek text of Revelation has undergone a drastic change in meaning: The transliteration of that word from Greek to English is *apocalupsis*. When we read or hear the anglicized version, *apocalypse*, the word *disaster* may flash on our mental screens. That's the common connotation of the word these days. If you Google "Define apocalypse," first, you are told it is "the complete and final destruction of the world, especially as described in the biblical book of Revelation." But that total destruction of the world does not happen in Revelation. The second definition is non-theological: "an event involving destruction or damage on an awesome or catastrophic scale." We could think, for example, of Marlon Brando and Martin Sheen's movie, *Apocalypse Now*, set in the catastrophic destruction of the Vietnam war. Only after those modern definitions does Google cite the origins of the Greek word: *uncovering* or *revealing*.

That is the biblical meaning: In Greek, *apocalypse* simply means *revelation*. So that very first word should tell us something is going to be revealed, made known, as we read further.

The First Five Words

We learn more about this *apocalypse* as the first five words of the book tell us this is *the revelation of Jesus Christ*. This can have double meaning: Chapter 1 basically reveals Jesus Christ. Then, all the remaining chapters of the book are the message Jesus Christ reveals to us. In the case of *apocalypse*, we need to forget the modern usage of the word and reclaim its biblical meaning.

Five More Words

Five other words in the first verse are crucial for our understanding. The author, writing nearly two thousand years ago, says he has received Christ's revelation of *what must soon take place*. Also, in verse 3, he says, *the time is near*. He says in 3:11 and three times at the end of the book in chapter 22, *I am coming soon* (22:7, 12, 20).

Misguided people try to make Revelation a roadmap to guide them through events at the end of the world as we know it. But if the book were about things in our time or later, why would the writer two millennia ago say he's going to tell *what must soon take place*?

Next, in verse 3, John indicates this is a circular letter to be read aloud in the churches:

Blessed is he who reads aloud the words of the prophecy, and blessed are those who hear, and who keep what is written therein; for the time is near.

Author and Audience (vv. 4a, 9-11)

We see another indication the book is intended for a first-century audience as the author identifies himself and his audience.

- His name is John (vv. 4a, 9).
- He is a fellow believer in Jesus who, with his audience, is enduring oppression or tribulation. He apparently is in exile on the island of Patmos because of his faithful witness to Jesus (v. 9).

He experiences awareness of God's Spirit in a time of perhaps private worship on Sunday, *the Lord's day* (vv. 10-11). The Spirit instructs him to write to seven specific churches in historically identifiable cities (in modern-day western Turkey), not to an abstract readership in some far-removed future era.

"Write what you see in a book and send it to the seven churches, to Ephesus and to Smyrna and to Pergamum and to Thyatira and to Sardis and to Philadelphia and to Laodicea.

Revelation, then, like the other twenty-six books of the New Testament, is written for people alive when the author wrote, addressing circumstances in the first century. We can find spiritual guidance on its pages today, just as people have done across the centuries. But we need first to understand what the folks back then were facing.

Revealing Jesus

Throughout the New Testament, Jesus receives superlative descriptions, and Revelation 1 is one of the richest in offering unqualified attributions.

The first of these is a trinitarian statement in verses 4-6:

Grace to you and peace from him who is and who was and who is to come, and from the seven spirits who are before his throne, and from Jesus Christ the faithful witness, the first-born of the dead, and the ruler of kings on earth. To him who loves us and has freed us from our sins by his blood and made us a kingdom, priests to his God and Father, to him be glory and dominion for ever and ever. Amen (vv. 4-6).

God the Father and the Holy Spirit are not named in so many words, but grace and peace are extended from all three members of the Trinity: God the Father is *him who is and who was and who is to come.* With the number *seven* a frequent symbol of completeness or perfection, we see the Holy Spirit in *the seven spirits who are before* [the Father's] *throne.*

John is especially fond of the number *seven.* We've already noted he is writing to *seven* churches. Now, in verses 5 and 6, he offers a *sevenfold* description of Jesus:

- He is *the faithful witness* to the power of God.
- He is *the first-born of the dead* as shown in His resurrection.
- He is all-powerful as *the ruler of kings on earth.*
- He is one *who loves us.*
- He *has freed us from our sins by his blood.*
- He has bestowed royalty on us as He *made us a kingdom.*
- He also has made us *priests to his God and Father,* people who go to God on behalf of others.

As we try to take in these seven superlatives, John declares Jesus will come with clouds of glory, seen by all humanity. Those who follow Him will rejoice, but others *will wail on account of him (verse 7).*

Then we hear a declaration from God the Father, as the one who has always been and always will be: *"I am the Alpha and the Omega* (the first and last letters of the Greek alphabet), *says the Lord*

God, who is and who was and who is to come, the Almighty"* (verse 8).

We've already noted the writer identifies himself and his audience (verses 9-11). At that point, John hears the voice behind him, commanding him to write to the churches.

John turns to see who is speaking, and we see further elaborate symbols pointing to the greatness of Jesus:

Then I turned to see the voice that was speaking to me, and on turning I saw seven golden lampstands, and in the midst of the lampstands one like a son of man, clothed with a long robe and with a golden girdle round his breast . . . (vv. 12-13)

"Son of Man" is from the Old Testament book of Daniel (7:13). Jesus uses the term several dozen times in the four Gospels to refer to Himself. The word has come to have messianic significance. Christ's standing among the lampstands is explained in verse 20.

This *one like a son of man* wears a long robe and golden girdle – the garb of the high priest, as prescribed in the Jewish Scriptures (Exodus 28). The New Testament book of Hebrews focuses on Christ as the Great High Priest. One of the chief functions of a priest is to make intercession – to pray to God – on behalf of the people. So Christ, the priest, stands among His churches, praying to God the Father for His churches.

Then comes another sevenfold description of Christ the Lord of the churches (vv. 14-16). We will see several of these descriptions again in chapters 2 and 3 in the letters to seven churches as Christ describes Himself. Here are the descriptions:

- *His head and his hair were white as white wool, white as snow.*

This also is from Daniel 7, describing a figure called the Ancient of Days. John uses the term to say Christ has existed from eternity. We also note, white symbolizes purity.

- *His eyes were like a flame of fire.*

This, too, is borrowed from Daniel (10:6). Fire penetrates and purifies all that survives the flame.

- *His feet were like burnished bronze, refined as in a furnace.*

Brass is a symbol of strength. So Christ stands in great strength.

- *And his voice was like the sound of many waters.*

If you've stood by a waterfall or on the coast and listened to the roar of the water, you probably have been struck by its might and power. So God speaks forcefully through Christ.

- *In his right hand he held seven stars.*

These stars are explained in verse 20 along with the seven golden lampstands.

- *From his mouth issued a sharp two-edged sword.*

Before the drama of Revelation is played out, that sword (in Christ's mouth, not in His hand) will play a crucial part in the battle against the forces of evil at Armageddon (19:15, 21).

- *And his face was like the sun shining in full strength.*

The sun is the brightest and strongest light known to humans. In the closing chapters (21:23; 22:5), describing the holy city, new Jerusalem, God and the Lamb are the light, removing any need for the sun or moon. Those churches needed assurance of light from God.

As he sees this vision of Christ, John is stricken with awe and fear (v. 17): *When I saw him, I fell at his feet as though dead.* But Christ wants John to be alive and alert (v. 18):

But he laid his right hand upon me, saying, 'Fear not, I am the first and the last, and the living one; I died, and behold I am alive for evermore, and I have the keys of Death and Hades.'

The *right hand* is generally considered the strong hand, the one commonly used in accomplishing what needs to be done.

Fear not echoes assurance from Jesus in the Gospels, including Matthew 10:31; Luke 5:10; Luke 8:50; Luke 12:32, John 12:15.

The declaration, *I am the first and the last*, repeats the assurance from God in verse 8, *I am the Alpha and the Omega.* This expression will occur twice more near the end of the book (21:6, 22:13), emphasizing God's eternal presence, the One in whom all things consist.

Further reassurance of Christ's resurrection comes as He tells John, *I died, and behold I am alive for evermore.*

The final assurance in this series says, *I have the keys of Death and Hades*. *Death and Hades* are riders on the fourth horse in chapter 6. This term also is a foreshadowing of 20:14, declaring Christ's power over death and the grave.

After these multiple assurances, Christ reminds John of his assignment:

Now write what you see, what is and what is to take place hereafter (v. 19)

Then the chapter closes in with the aforementioned explanation of the stars and lampstands:

As for the mystery of the seven stars which you saw in my right hand, and the seven golden lampstands, the seven stars are the angels of the seven churches and the seven lampstands are the seven churches (v. 20).

So Christ holding the seven pastors [the stars] in His strong right hand means He protects them as they lead the churches. These are the churches He will write letters to in chapters 2 and 3, urging them to avoid various temptations such as burning incense to the Roman emperor or falling prey to materialism or going through the form of worship without the spirit or succumbing to heresy.

Safe in the Arms of Jesus

In the spirit of John's assurance in this opening first century vision in Revelation, Fanny J. Crosby, the blind hymn writer who lived in the nineteenth century, expressed the security of being held by Jesus Christ in the song, "Safe in the Arms of Jesus":

Safe in the arms of Jesus, Safe from corroding care,
Safe from the world's temptations; Sin cannot harm me there.
Free from the blight of sorrow, Free from my doubts and fears;
Only a few more trials, Only a few more tears!
Safe in the arms of Jesus, Safe on His gentle breast;
There by His love o'ershaded, Sweetly my soul shall rest.[1]

2 – Revelation, Chapters 2-3: Letters to Seven Churches

Background

With digital technology, it's easy to set up a standard letter to send to several people and then make changes to personalize the message for individual recipients. When John wrote Revelation, he didn't have a computer or even a typewriter. Still, he envisioned a message to include early in the book in the form of letters to seven different churches. Then, as he wrote by hand, he adapted that general message to apply to each individual congregation.

In chapter 1, John is told to write what he is about to see and send it to seven churches. Chapters 2 and 3 are letters from Jesus to those churches. They follow a sevenfold framework, but John makes changes with each church:

1) Each letter begins: *To the angel* [pastor] *of the church at* _____ *write . . .*
2) Each letter includes a unique self-description of Christ for each church.
3) To most of the churches, Jesus says, *I know your works.*
4) The *I know* usually introduces a commendation.
5) For three churches, the commendation is followed by *But I have this against you.*
6) A call to be spiritually sensitive: *He who has an ear, let him hear what the Spirit says to the churches.*
7) Promises of eternal bliss if they remain true and conquer in His name.

John names seven specific churches, so with number seven symbolizing completeness, we might think of these messages as for all churches of that era and, by extension, all churches for all time.

Revelation was a circular document for the seven churches on the western side of present day Turkey near the Aegean Sea. The seven cities, in the order the letters appear in the text, form a kind of horseshoe. This geographic pattern would expedite sending the entire book from church to church after each church read the letter and made a copy for its own use. The island of Patmos, where John apparently was in exile, was in the Aegean southwest of Ephesus.

Among those who interpret Revelation as essentially end-time prophecy, some say each church in sequence represents chronological periods of church history. A quick search of the Internet will lead to sites supporting this view. Some of these provide charts listing specific dates of church history for each church and characterizing what we might call "the state of the church" in each period. This seems contrived because, with the passing of years, when the end does not come, the seven periods have to be stretched to fit each generation, with the age of Laodicea, a church in urgent need of repentance, always including the period in which this interpretation is given.

Also, we need to ask again, what relevance would a wide sweep of churches in far-away time periods have for the struggling churches of Asia Minor in the first Christian century?

The Churches

Old Testament scholar Walter Brueggemann has discerned a motif in both Old and New Testaments that has relevance for our study of Revelation's seven churches. For decades, Dr. Brueggemann has written, lectured and preached on how people of faith find themselves in tension with the larger population or with hostile authorities in the empire or with both.

In his 1978 book, *The Prophetic Imagination*, he speaks of a "dominant culture" that seeks to dull or mute the prophetic voice and domesticate the people of God. The prophet's challenge is to "nurture, nourish, and evoke a consciousness and perception alternative to the consciousness and perception of the dominant culture around us."[2] The prophet calls God's people "to live in fervent anticipation of the newness that God has promised and will surely give."[3]

Brueggemann notes the recurring need to confront the empire in the ministry and witness of Moses, the prophets, and Jesus Himself. Moses makes "a radical break with the social reality of Pharaoh's Egypt,"[4] demanding that the Egyptian ruler "let my people go" (Exodus 5:1; 10:4).

Israel as a distinct people came into being when Moses was allowed to lead his people out of Egypt. After their wilderness wandering and their conquest of their Promised Land, the Israelites were led for a time by charismatic judges, then by kings. Then a sad, ironic pattern developed. The kings of Israel and Judah established their own "dominant culture," frequently setting up altars to pagan gods. This provoked Amos, Micah, and Isaiah to challenge the "dominant culture" and their own imperial leaders who turned from the God of Abraham, Isaac, and Jacob.

In the New Testament, the message and ministry of Jesus unfolds under the domination of the pagan Roman Empire.

Though Brueggemann does not include Revelation in his analysis of the dominant culture and the force of empire, he could well have done so. John is on Patmos, separated from the churches *on account of the word of God and the testimony of Jesus*. Their daily challenge is to distinguish themselves from the dominant culture and to stay true to their Lord under threats from representatives of the empire. The entire book deals with these issues Brueggemann has delineated.

Several of the churches already are under severe persecution for refusing to burn incense at Caesar's altars, in acknowledgment of the emperor and the empire. Other churches apparently are trying to have it both ways as they "go along to get along" with the dominant culture. One congregation — the last one — seems to be living comfortably as they have made peace with the culture.

Each letter includes evaluation of how the church is dealing with these issues. Several letters include stern admonition. But each concludes with encouragement.

We may think of these letters as report cards, with two churches getting A's for faithfulness, four getting C's, and one getting an F. We will look at the C's first, then the A's, and finally the F.

Ephesus (2:1-7) Grade: C

We will get an understanding of the seven-fold formula for all the letters by examining that structure in detail in the letter to Ephesus:

1) *To the angel* [pastor] *of the church at Ephesus write* . . . (and so with each church)
2) There is a unique self-description of Christ for each church. Except for Philadelphia, these descriptions are picked up from chapter 1. Here is the description for Ephesus : *The words of him who holds the seven stars in his right hand, who walks among the seven golden lampstands.*

We learned in chapter 1 that *star* is a symbol for *pastor* and a *lampstand* is another word for *church*. So Christ actively cares for His pastors and the churches.

3) To all but Smyrna and Pergamum, Jesus says, *I know your works*.
4) *I know* introduces a commendation for all but Laodicea. To Ephesus, He says, *I know your works, your toil and your patient endurance, and how you cannot bear evil men but have tested those who call themselves apostles but are not, and found them to be false. I know you are enduring patiently and bearing up for my name's sake, and you have not grown weary.*
5) For Ephesus, Pergamum, and Thyatira, the commendation is followed by words such as these: *But I have this against you.* He has this against Ephesus: *You have abandoned the love you had at first. Remember then from what you have fallen, repent and do the works you did at first. If not, I will come to you and remove your lampstand from its place, unless you repent.*

They are hard working and patient. They've stood up to members who aren't what they claim to be. So what brings Christ's rebuke? It comes to this: Despite working hard and enduring hardship as they rooted out the unfaithful, they no longer have a loving spirit. They've gotten so wrapped up in enforcement that they forget the ultimate way of love.

Still, Christ does not finish with the Ephesians on that negative note. He says, *Yet this you have, you hate the works of the Nicolaitans, which I also hate*. The Nicolaitans are not identified in the New Testament, but scholars suggest they are a Christian sect who accommodate to the emperor, making sacrifice before his statue.

With the following identical words, all seven churches are called to be spiritually sensitive:
He who has an ear, let him hear what the Spirit says to the churches.

To all seven churches, no matter how wayward, Christ extends promises of eternal bliss if they remain true and conquer in His name. For Ephesus: *To him who conquers I will grant to eat of the tree of life, which is in the paradise of God.*

Pergamum (2:12-17)   Grade: C

For Pergamum, Christ is the one *who has the sharp two-edged sword in His mouth*. It is His word of power, even in Pergamum, *where Satan dwells*. The this harsh designation refers to the temples to Caesar Augustus and to the city of Rome. There also were temples to Zeus, Athena, Dionysius, and Asklepios. Because it is the administrative center of Asia, it thus is the center for enforcement of emperor worship.

Christ gives good marks because *you hold fast my name and you did not deny my faith even in the days of Antipas my witness, my faithful one, who was killed among you, where Satan dwells*. Antipas was a member of the the Pergamum church, who died rather than worship the emperor (2:13).

Despite these strong points, Christ says, *I have a few things against you.* He cites two groups of false teachers who lead people to sacrifice to the emperor: the Nicolaitans, as in Ephesus, and also some *who hold the teachings of Balaam* [an unfaithful Israelite prophet] *who taught Balak to put a stumbling block before the sons of Israel* (Numbers, chapters 22-23).

Still, there is hope for the faithful: *hidden manna*, nourishment such as God provided the Israelites during their wilderness wanderings; and *a white stone, with a new name written on the stone which no one knows except him who receives it.* The white stone is in contrast with charms containing names of pagan deities.

Thyatira (2:18-29) Grade: C

Writing to the third church to receive both positive and negative words, Christ tells Thyatira He is *the Son of God, who has eyes like a flame of fire, and whose feet are like burnished bronze* (2:18).

Son of God is such a familiar term in the New Testament, we may let it slide by. But this allusion to Daniel 10:6 is a designation of Christ's authority. The fiery eyes can penetrate to the depth and discern unfaithful hearts. Feet of brass represent strength.

Similar to Ephesus and Pergamum, Thyatira has faithful members as well as some who lead others astray. The deceitful leader in Thyatira is a woman Christ calls Jezebel. In 1 Kings, chapter 16, Queen Jezebel in the Northern Kingdom establishes worship of the false god, Baal. Thyatira's Jezebel *is teaching and beguiling my servants to practice immorality* [adultery] *and to eat food sacrificed to idols.* Adultery here is spiritual unfaithfulness, as Jezebel leads fellow church members to burn incense to Caesar. Unless the church repents, Christ will bring severe judgment on Jezebel and strike her children dead.

Even so, Christ acknowledges there are faithful Christians in Thyatira, urging them, *only hold fast what you have, until I come. He who conquers and who keeps my works until the end, I will give him power over the nations, and he shall rule them with a rod of iron . . . and I will give him the morning star.*

In Daniel, righteous people shine like stars in heaven (12:3). Later in Revelation, Christ Himself is the bright morning star

(22:16) who lights the way for His people.

Sardis (3:1-6) Grade: C-

Sardis is the fourth and final church to get bad words and good ones. But here, harsh words are predominant. Christ *has the seven spirits of God and the seven stars. Seven spirits* reminds them that God's perfect Spirit is present to search their hearts and give them new life. Jesus says, *you have the name of being alive, and you are dead.*

But then, He softens that statement: Instead of being dead, they are asleep: *If you will not wake up, I will come like a thief, and you will not know at what hour I will come upon you.*

Industries in Sardis included manufacture of woolen garments. So Christ commends those *who have not soiled their garments.* And *He who conquers shall be clad thus in white garments, and I will not blot his name out of the book of life; I will confess his name before my Father and before his angels.* (3:4-5).

With the soiled reputation of this church, it is ironic that Sardis is a popular name for rural churches in the South. Another example of lack of careful reading of Revelation!

Smyrna (2:8-11) Grade: A

Smyrna is one of the two churches (with Philadelphia) for whom Christ offers no criticism. To Smyrna, Christ is *the first and the last, who died and came to life.* The eternal Christ who died and rose again offers assurance in the face of threefold suffering: *I know your tribulation and your poverty (but you are rich) and the slander of those who say that they are Jews and are not, but are a synagogue of Satan* (2:9).

They have suffered for Christ, and they should expect more: *The devil is about to throw some of you into prison, that you may be tested, and for ten days you will have tribulation. Be faithful unto death, and I will give you the crown of life* (2:10).

The number ten also is a symbol of completeness in Revelation, so the ten days of tribulation are not a literal week and a half.

Rather, the Smyrnans can expect thorough persecution for the sake of Christ, even to death. But those who die for Christ will receive crowns of life and need not fear the second death which awaits those who reject God (2:11).

Later, in chapter 7, a countless number of the faithful come out of great tribulation. God's faithful people undergoing great tribulation seem to undermine the popular expectation that Christians will be snatched out of the world in the Rapture and escape the Great Tribulation.

Philadelphia (3:7-13) Grade: A

Philadelphia is the other church who receives only praise. To the Philadelphians, Christ presents Himself as *the holy one, the true one, who has the key of David, who opens and no one shall shut, who shuts and no one opens.* The Holy One of Israel was a messianic figure in the Hebrew Scriptures. The key of David is also a messianic reference. In Isaiah, chapter 22, it is prophesied that a man named Eliakim will receive the key of the house of David. So, Christ promises the Philadelphia church a key to open a door no one can shut.

The Philadelphians have suffered at the hands of Jews. Recall that as the Christian movement separated from its Jewish roots, both Jesus and Paul faced ongoing difficulties with Jewish leaders. That conflict continues in the time of Revelation, but Christ promises victory.

They have suffered and remained faithful, and widespread trials are still to come. But Christ promises He is coming soon (3:11), so the Philadelphians are urged to *hold fast what you have, so that no one may seize your crown.* Those who conquer in the face of harsh trials will be strong pillars *in the temple of my God.* The temple in Jerusalem had been destroyed by the time Revelation was written, so this symbolically promises the faithful will remain in God's presence.

Christ will write a threefold name on the obedient Christian, foreshadowing the promise of the seal placed on God's people in chapter 7. This seal is in contrast with the infamously misunderstood mark of the beast in chapter 13. As we progress, we will see how end-of-the-worlders build an elaborate, fearful system around the Beast and his mark. But here, the faithful will have *the name of my God, and the name of the city of my God, the new Jerusalem which comes down from my God out of heaven, and my own new name.* The climax of the entire vision of Revelation is this new Jerusalem coming down out of heaven in chapter 21.

Laodicea (3:14-22) Grade: F

We noted there are many Sardis churches, named after a disobedient church, but you've probably never heard of a congregation named for Laodicea. Christ offers them no commendation. Their sin is reliance on physical and financial comfort.

I know your works: you are neither cold nor hot. Would that you were cold or hot! So, because you are lukewarm, and neither cold nor hot, I will spew you out of my mouth.

Christ comes to this indifferent church as *the Amen, the faithful and true witness, the beginning of God's creation.*

Amen speaks of verification of truth, so *the Amen, the faithful and true witness* is double guarantee the hearers can trust what is being said. The third descriptor, Christ as *the beginning of God's creation*, calls to mind John 1:2-3: *He was in the beginning with God; all things were made through him, and without him was not anything made that was made.*

Laodicea, as a center of banking and finance, clothing manufacturing, and medicine for the ears and eyes, could boast it was rich. Church members joined in the boast: *I am rich, I have prospered, and I need nothing.* But Christ says they don't know they really *are wretched, pitiable, poor, blind, and naked.*

These descriptions contrast with the elements which made the city great:

- Wretched, pitiable, and poor in the shadow of the financial district.

- Blind despite the availability of ointment for the eyes.
- Naked in a city of clothing manufacturers.

Christ offers remedies: *Therefore I counsel you to buy from me gold refined by fire, that you may be rich, and white garments to clothe you and to keep the shame of your nakedness from being seen, and salve to anoint your eyes, that you may see.*

All seven letters stress Christ loves and cares for His churches. But He reminds smug, conceited Laodicea: love can involve punishment: *Those whom I love, I reprove and chasten* (3:19). He calls them to *be zealous and repent.*

The letter that starts with harsh rebuke ends with an invitation and plea:

Behold, I stand at the door and knock; if any one hears my voice and opens the door, I will come in to him and eat with him, and he with me (3:20).

He makes a promise to each church. To Laodicea, if they repent and thus conquer evil, *I will grant him to sit with me on my throne, as I myself conquered and sat down with my Father on his throne.*

Christ's love shines through, even for Laodicea. It's not too late for those who repent.

Stand Up, Stand Up For Jesus

George Duffiled's song, "Stand Up, Stand Up for Jesus," from 1858 picks up on the challenges to these early churches:

Stand up, stand up for Jesus; The strife will not be long;
This day the noise of battle, The next the victor's song.
To him that overcometh, A crown of life shall be
And with the King of glory Shall reign eternally.[5]

Now, it's on to the vision Christ has given John.

3 – Revelation, Chapters 4-5: A Vision Before the Vision

Billy Graham led a month-long crusade in Louisville, Kentucky, in 1956. This was early in my first semester of seminary. Many of us students attended the evangelistic services as often as we felt we could without jeopardizing our grades. The Graham meeting "baptized" or "christened" Freedom Hall, as the first major user of the facility.

At full capacity, Freedom Hall will seat some 19,000. I've been to larger venues, including major league baseball stadiums, but the Graham crusade in Freedom Hall in 1956, often near capacity, was – and still is – the largest church service I have ever attended.

Chapters 4-5 depict a massive worship gathering, focusing on *the one seated on the throne* and on *a Lamb standing, as though it had been slain*. Worshipers include representatives of all creatures of the earth. Then, numberless throngs join in praise to the Lamb, making cumulative attendance at all evangelistic crusades and sporting events minuscule by comparison.

All this as final preparation for the major *apocalypse*, the major revelation.

The Pre-Vision Vision

An unseen speaker with a voice like a trumpet invites John up into heaven through an open door: *Come up here, and I will show you what must take place after this* (v. 1). In time sequence, this comes immediately after the vision of Christ in chapter 1 (with the letters in chapters 2-3 an interlude).

Five things to notice in chapters 4-5:
- John catches a glimpse of an unidentified *one seated on the throne*.
- All the creatures in heaven endlessly sing praise to the *one*

seated on the throne.
- *The one seated on the throne* holds a scroll with important writing, but no one can be found who is worthy to open the scroll.
- There appears a Lamb who had been slain. He is declared worthy to open the scroll and reveal what is to happen.
- Every creature in heaven, on earth, under the earth, and in the sea praises the Lamb (5:13). Perhaps this all-inclusive worship anticipates that ultimate day when *at the name of Jesus every knee should bow, in heaven and on earth and under the earth, and every tongue confess that Jesus Christ is Lord, to the glory of God the Father* (Philippians 2:10-11). This sets the stage for the Lamb to open the seals in chapter 6, unleashing the elaborate series of visions comprising the rest of the book.

The *one seated on the throne* obviously is God, but John gives no description of God. Rather John simply compares God to the brightness of precious stones, *jasper and carnelian, and . . . a rainbow that looked like an emerald* (4:3). This is a reminder that we can experience God, but our knowledge of God is limited. Our ability to describe God is limited. Someone has said, "The God we talk about is One who really cannot be talked about." However much we may know of God, there is always infinitely more to know. In Isaiah's vision (Isaiah 6), the Lord is high and lifted up, hidden in glory, but, as here in Revelation, Isaiah does not attempt to describe God.

Not only does John refuse to try to describe God, in this scene, he will not even say God's name. God is simply the *one seated on the throne!* This unwillingness to speak God's name is consistent with long-standing reverence for the Holy Name which led Jews to use the substitute name Adonai rather than Yahweh, God's name revealed to Moses (Exodus 3:14).

Today, as Jewish religion writers publish in English, we often see this reservation about using the Divine Name as they write G-d instead of God. Some scribes in ancient times, who copied manuscripts of the Jewish Bible by hand, were said to stop writing when they came to the Divine Name. They would clean their writing pens before writing that Name.

So here in Revelation, John is filled with reverence before *the one seated on the throne*, who cannot be described and whose name cannot be uttered.

Twenty-Four Elders

After the vision of the *one seated on the throne*, John sees heavenly creatures who unceasingly sing praise to God. First we see twenty-four elders (4:4) who have been interpreted as representing the heads of the twelve tribes of Israel and the twelve apostles, suggesting the old and new covenants – in modern terminology, the Old and New Testaments. The twenty-four elders, dressed in white robes and wearing golden crowns, are seated on thrones. The crowns and thrones indicate they are kings in their own right, but verse 10 says they cast their crowns before God. These men who loom large in Jewish Scripture and in the Christian Gospels are near the throne, but they know their place is to sing praise to God constantly, claiming no recognition or honor for themselves.

As the twenty-four elders sit on their lesser thrones around the one great throne, *From the throne issue flashes of lightning, and voices and peals of thunder* (v. 5) – signs of God's power.

There also are seven flaming torches in front of the throne. These seven flames are the seven spirits of God. With seven suggesting completeness or perfection, the seven spirits indicate the Holy Spirit of God is all-powerful and ever-present.

[B]efore the throne there is as it were a sea of glass, like crystal (v. 6). That expression *as it were* means something before the throne resembling *sea*. This suggests the shining brilliance of God, a brilliance blinding mortals who come near, and also a barrier indicating we dare not, we cannot, come too close to God.

Theologians use two contrasting words to describe God. *Transcendent* means God is high above us. On the other hand, *imma-*

nence refers to God's revealing Himself in a close, personal way to humanity. In Christian Scripture, we see both God's immanence – real and personal in Christ – but also transcendence – the God who made all things, in whom we live and move and have our being. This scene in the heavenly throne room emphasizes God's transcendence, separated from his creatures by something like a glassy sea.

Four Living Creatures

A quartet calling themselves Revelation Four sang at a Gospel music festival sponsored by Lions Clubs in South Carolina. I asked them whether their name might be related to Revelation, chapter four. All four of the young Lions are Christians and active churchmen, but they confessed they knew little about Revelation and nothing specific about chapter 4. They simply wanted their singing to be a revelation of God, and there were four of them, so they came up with the Revelation Four name.

I suggested, if they were to read Revelation 4, they would discover a significant connection: In verses 8-9, there are four living creatures who day and night *never cease to sing, "Holy, holy, holy, is the Lord God Almighty, who was and is and is to come."* Chapters 4 and 5 are almost non-stop singing.

The four singers in these chapters appear at strategic points throughout the book (4:6-9; 5:6-11; 6:1-7; 7:11; 14:3; 15:7; and 19:4). Their primary activity is praise to *him who is seated on the throne, who lives for ever and ever.* We might think of their modern counterparts as ministers of music in churches who lead choirs, ensembles, and congregations in praise to God.

These strange creatures are the first of many fantasy figures in Revelation. They are *full of eyes in front and behind, the first living creature like a lion, the second living creature like an ox, the third living creature with the face of a man, and the fourth living creature like a flying eagle. And the four living creatures, each of them with six wings, are full of eyes all round and within* (4:6-8).

They represent all living, breathing creatures of earth and sky:

the lion equals wild beasts; the ox, tame animals; man, the highest of all the creatures; and the eagle, bird life. These creatures' songs have inspired many other songs across the centuries. One example is St. Francis's song in the thirteenth century: "All creatures of our God and King, lift up your voice and with us sing, alleluia."[6]

In this century, in the spirit of array of creatures in Revelation, Bill Staines's lighthearted, spirited song, "A Place in the Choir," has become popular on the Internet and in churches. It declares, "All God's creatures have a place in the choir," with a variety of animals singing low and higher. Staines's songsters range from a hoot owl to a porcupine, from dogs and cats to a honeybee, from a bullfrog to a hippopotamus, from a cricket to an alligator.[7]

The song by Revelation's four living creatures inspires the twenty-four elders to fall down before God and sing: "You are worthy, our Lord and God, to receive glory and honour and power, for you created all things, and by your will they existed and were created."

So Revelation 4 points to God, who is beyond our sight, beyond our understanding, with the four living creatures leading everyone in praise to this *one who sits on the throne*.

The Scroll And The Lamb

In chapter 5, the *one on the throne* holds a scroll, and the message fills both the front and the back of the scroll. Usually writing would be only on the inside. In modern terms, it is as if the message is so urgent, the writer uses the paper inside and then writes on the envelope.

Third, the scroll is perfectly sealed with seven seals, so no one can know its contents.

The air of expectancy and excitement increases when *a strong angel calls out with a loud voice, "Who is worthy to open the scroll and break its seals?"* (v. 2)

John, as a spectator, is caught up in the excitement, wondering who can open the scroll. Then he hears bad news: no one in heaven or on earth or under the earth was able to open the scroll or to look into it. This causes him to weep much. But then comes the triumphal announcement:

One of the elders uses popular titles from Jewish Scripture as he tells John, *"Do not weep. See the Lion of the tribe of Judah, the Root of David, has conquered so that he can open the scroll and its seven seals"* (v. 5).

This is the first announcement of Christ's triumph – the central message of Revelation: Victory is declared before we even learn of the battle God's people will face. All hell will break loose in the anticipated vision, but we hear the assuring word up front: Christ has conquered, so He can open the scroll and its seven seals.

John is eager to see this great Lion of the tribe of Judah. But he sees something quite different: *Then I saw between the throne and the four living creatures and among the elders a Lamb standing as if it had been slain* (v. 6).

The slain Lamb is in other books of the Bible. In John 1:29, Jesus is *the Lamb of God who takes away the sin of the world.* In Revelation 13, He is *the Lamb slain from the foundation of the world.*

But Jesus is no ordinary lamb. He has seven horns and seven eyes. His seven horns symbolize perfect power, and seven eyes symbolize perfect knowledge. This perfect knowledge is embodied in *the seven spirits of God sent out into all the earth.* We noted earlier, the seven spirits denote God's perfect Spirit. So, once again, we have the threefold manifestation of God: the Father, the one who sits on the throne; Jesus, the Lamb who was slain; and the seven spirits of God, the perfect Holy Spirit.

The Lamb shows His worthiness as he takes the scroll from the hand of God (v. 7).

A Gigantic Worship Service

The remaining verses of Revelation 5 celebrate Jesus, the Lamb, who will open the seals on the scroll in the next chapter and reveal times of tribulation but also ultimate triumph for the faithful ones of God. The Lamb has already conquered.

Some people like to get a book and go to the end to see how it comes out before reading the early parts, even though that takes away any suspense. It's like that here, as those early Christians are told the outcome of the great distress some of them are already enduring: The Lamb has conquered.

In verse 8, as the Lamb takes the scroll, *the four living creatures and the twenty-four elders [fall] before the Lamb, each holding a harp and golden bowls full of incense, which are the prayers of the saints.* Then the four living creatures and the twenty-four elders sing a new song, declaring the Lamb worthy to open the seals and reveal the message because His death has ransomed God's people from around the world (v. 9): *You are worthy to take the scroll and to open its seals, for you were slaughtered and by your blood you ransomed for God saints from every tribe and language and people and nation.*

The four living creatures and the twenty-four elders are joined by angels in such a large crowd that author John cannot begin to count everyone at worship. He uses the Greek word *muriades*, which transliterates into English as *myriad*: an innumerable multitude, an unlimited number. He says there are *myriads of myriads and thousands of thousands*. To try to describe the crowd in heaven, John starts with myriads, a crowd too big to count. Then he tries to multiply that first impossible number by another unlimited number. Then that multiplied number is multiplied again by thousands of thousands, with the word *chiliades* for thousands. Think of the largest number you can think possible, then add one. It's simply impossible to count.

All these heavenly beings sing with full voice, *"Worthy is the Lamb that was slain, to receive power and wealth and wisdom and might and honour and glory and blessing!"* (v. 12)

But this song of praise to the Lamb doesn't stop with the numberless crowd in heaven. Every creature imaginable joins in praise to God and to Christ:

Then I heard every creature in heaven and on earth and under the earth and in the sea, and all that is in them, singing, "To the one seated on the throne and to the Lamb be blessing and honour and glory and might for ever and ever" (v. 13).

The songs of praise to God and to Christ in these chapters have inspired other songs, ranging from the contemporary praise song, "Worthy of Worship" to "Worthy is the Lamb," the climactic closing choral number in George Frederick Handel's *Messiah*.

This triumphant scene in chapters 4-5 ends as we come back to those four singers, the four living creatures. They're singing again. This time, they simply say, *Amen*, which means, "Yes. Yes. Let it be so." At that, the twenty-four elders fall down and worship.

Once again, this scene celebrates the victory Christ the Lamb has already won. This is a message of hope as the churches are facing tribulation – persecution at the hands of the Roman government because they refuse to worship the emperor as god.

When the worthy Lamb starts opening the seals in chapter 6, we will get into vivid imagery depicting the great struggle as the forces of evil make war against the First Century church.

O Thou In Whose Presence

Joseph Swain's song, "O Thou in Whose Presence," written in 1791, recalls the song sung by myriads:

> *"O Thou in whose presence my soul takes delight,*
> *On whom in affliction I call;*
> *My comfort by day and my song in the night,*
> *My hope, my salvation, my all. . . .*
>
> *He looks, and ten thousand of angels rejoice,*
> *And myriads now wait for His word;*
> *He speaks, and eternity, filled with His voice,*
> *Re-echoes the praise of the Lord."*[8]

4 – Revelation, Chapters 6-11: Seven Seals and Seven Trumpets

Revelation As Drama

I love theater and have spent many enjoyable and edifying evenings in the audience, on stage, and in the wings as director. I use the term *edifying* deliberately because I often have found food for thought and even Christian inspiration from secular drama.

With my interest in theater, I have been fascinated to see many scholars from the mid-twentieth century to the present approach Revelation as a drama. This seems highly appropriate because of the visions and spectacles that explode from its pages, beginning with chapter 6 and building with intensity through most of the rest of the book.

Two authors who develop the drama motif most extensively are John Wick Bowman in *The Drama of the Book of Revelation*[9] and James L. Blevins in *Revelation as Drama*.[10] Both divide Revelation into seven acts, with seven scenes in each act.

In chapters 6, 8, and 9 of Revelation, people panic and run for cover as the world is falling apart. Perhaps we can see a dramatic parallel between widespread destruction and chaos in these chapters and in the classic Broadway musical *Cabaret*. Destruction in Revelation is on a cosmic scale while *Cabaret* depicts chaos largely in the lives of a few individuals, but there is overarching evil in each case: the oppressive hand of the Roman emperor in Revelation and the rising threat of Adolf Hitler in the musical.

Principal characters in *Cabaret* are two romantic couples: A young British singer at the cabaret and her American beau share a bed. She becomes pregnant, then has an abortion, and they break up. Under the gathering cloud of anti-semitism, a middle-aged German woman ends her relationship with her suitor because he is a Jew. So, at the final curtain, the lives of all these central characters are in shambles.[11]

When a touring company was performing *Cabaret* in Atlanta during Holy Week in 1969, a reporter asked an actress whether it was appropriate to do the show during Lent. Signe Hasso, who portrayed the pragmatic-minded older woman, said, "I hope that people come to see *Cabaret*, then go to church and hear about the resurrection, symbolizing good." She said we must be able to recognize evil in order to recognize good.[12]

Even though this present book does not develop the drama concept as such, dramatic elements abound throughout Revelation, with larger-than-life characters waiting in the wings to take center stage as the curtain rises on chapter 6. So we might say, "On with the show!"

Two Parallel Passages

Amid pageantry and visions, chapters 6-11 depict God's sustaining care in the midst of judgment and destruction. This message unfolds in two passages with parallel structure, the first in chapters 6-7, the second in chapters 8-11.

The action we had anticipated in chapter 5 begins in chapter 6: The Lamb who was slain begins opening the seven seals. The first four seals are opened in rapid succession, with brief depictions of four horsemen. Next come more detailed pictures with the fifth and sixth seals. With the fifth seal, we see martyred souls under the altar; with the sixth seal comes destruction in nature. Then, the opening of the seventh and final seal is interrupted with an interlude.

When the seventh seal is finally opened (8:1), it points to a new series of visions – these involving the sounding of seven trumpets. These continue through chapters 8-11. As with the seals, the first four trumpets sound in rapid succession, in this case with brief depictions of disruption of nature. Again, as with the fifth and sixth seals, the fifth and sixth trumpets usher in more elaborate scenes. These depict two destructive armies, the first an army of locusts, the second a human army of two hundred million cavalrymen. The parallel structure continues as the seventh trumpet is delayed by an elaborate interlude. When, at last, the seventh trumpet sounds, it is with announcement of God's triumphant reign over all the kingdoms of earth. Here, we visualize the parallel passages:

Seven Seals (6:1-8:1)	Seven Trumpets (8:2-11:19)
(1) White horse	(1) hail, fire, blood fall; 1/3 of earth and trees burn up
(2) Red horse	(2) 1/3 of sea becomes blood, 1/3 of sea creatures die, 1/3 of ships destroyed
(3) Black horse	(3) Wormwood star falls: 1/3 waters bitter; many men die
(4) Pale horse	(4) 1/3 of sun, moon, stars dark; 1/3 day, night light shines
(5) Martyrs under altar	(5) Locust army rises out of the earth
(6) Destruction in nature	(6) 200 million human army; 1/3 mankind killed
Interlude	Interlude
(7) Silence in heaven	(7) Declaration: The kingdom of this world has become the kingdom of our Lord and of his Christ

Chapters 6-7

A Football Analogy

Sports writer Grantland Rice in *The New York Herald Tribune* years ago dubbed members of the backfield of the Notre Dame football team "the Four Horsemen." Rice said the quartet visited "Famine, Pestilence, Destruction and Death" upon a team from West Point.

Coached by Notre Dame legend Knute Rockne, the backfielders' real names were Harry Stuhldreher, Don Miller, Jim Crowley and Elmer Layden.

Rice mixed metaphors in his article of October 18, 1924, as he went on to call the Fighting Irish team a cyclone that swept their Army opponents over the precipice at New York City's Polo Grounds.[13]

Irish fans keep the Horsemen designation alive: Their likenesses can be purchased online in an "officially licensed, limited edition" bronze sculpture, along with banners, flags, and decals.[14]

The Four Horsemen figure is drawn from Revelation, chapter 6.

The First Four Seals

Chapter 6 opens with the biblical four horsemen riding onto the scene as the Lamb takes the scroll from the hand of *the one seated on the throne* and begins opening the seven seals. Sportswriter Rice's precise IDs of "Famine, Pestilence, Destruction and Death" for the horsemen are not borrowed directly from Revelation, but the biblical scene is indeed filled with these elements.

One by one, as the first four seals are opened (vv. 1-8), the four living creatures we met in the previous chapters call forth horses of different colors. The rider on each horse brings increasing destruction – and finally death. They depict four stages of warfare: conquest, bloodshed, famine, and widespread death.

First, a white horse carries a mighty warrior who is intent on conquering weaker armies. He has a bow and wears a crown as he rides on his quest.

A bright red horse is next, with red symbolizing bloodshed. Its rider has a sword, and he is *permitted to take peace from the earth, so that men should slay one another.*

Third comes a black horse. Its rider brings scarcity of food and high prices for whatever food is available.

Finally, the fourth is a pale horse:

And its rider's name was Death, and Hades [the mythological realm of the dead] *followed him; and they were given power over a fourth of the earth, to kill with sword and with famine and with pestilence and by wild beasts of the earth.*

God's judgment can be seen in these riders. Not that God sends war, famine, and death. Neither does God prevent consequences of humanity's sinful actions against other mortals. War is always the result of breakdown in relations between nations. It results in destruction of cities and villages and natural resources; massive deaths and maimed bodies among survivors.

The Fifth And Six Seals

As the Lamb opens the fifth seal, the scene changes to the altar of God. We see *under the altar the souls of those who had been slain for the word of God and for the witness they had borne.*

These martyrs cry out for vengeance, but they are given white robes of purity and are *told to rest a little longer, until the number of their fellow servants and their brethren should be complete, who were to be killed as they themselves had been.*

Let's note a couple of things before the sixth seal is opened.

- The fifth seal takes us back to chapters 2-3 to the letters to the Smyrna and Philadelphia churches who have suffered for their faith. There, Christ also warns them to expect more. Now, more suffering and death has come to those who refuse to burn incense to Caesar.
- With the instruction to *rest a little longer* comes a reminder that human time may not coincide with God's time. God's patience is infinite; ours is not.

The sixth seal brings home the need for more patient endurance amid phenomenal natural disaster (vv. 12-17): *there was a great earthquake; and the sun became black as sackcloth, the full moon became like blood, and the stars of the sky fell to the earth as the fig tree sheds its winter fruit when shaken by a gale; the sky vanished like a scroll that is rolled up, and every mountain and island was removed from its place.*

John is inspired by Hebrew prophets in listing these cataclysmic events: Haggai describes an earthquake (2:6-7); in Joel the sun is darkened and the moon turns to blood (2:31); and Isaiah sees the sky roll up like a scroll and stars fall to earth (34:4).

All people of the earth are terrified: kings, great men, generals, the rich and strong, along with slave and free. Fearing *him who is seated on the throne, and the wrath of the Lamb* they call for the rocks and mountains to fall on them as lesser punishment. As the great day of wrath has come, they ask, *and who can stand before it?*

The Seventh Seal? Not Yet

Logically, as we move into chapter 7, the Lamb should now open the seventh and final seal on the scroll. Instead, in a pattern we will see again in chapters 8-11, a multifaceted vision interrupts completion of the series. Chapter 7 depicts two different groups of God's people.

Before we see these groups, an angel *from the rising of the sun* (the east) warns four other angels not to let damaging winds harm the earth and sea and trees *till we have sealed the servants of our God upon their foreheads"* (7:2-3).

In the pre-scientific flat earth understanding, good winds blew directly from north, east, south, and west, but contrary winds came from the corners. God's servants were to be protected from the ill winds until they received God's seal on their foreheads.

Ancient kings had rings they used for certifying important documents. Typically, the ring bore an icon associated with the king. The identifying mark was dipped into hot wax, and the wax then was used to seal the document, authenticating its origin. In John's vision, the sealing is not for parchment documents but for living documents: God's faithful servants.

The first group (verses 2-8) are those who receive the seal of God on their foreheads. There are one hundred forty-four thousand, consisting of twelve thousand from each of the twelve tribes of Israel. Interpreters who read Revelation as the literal unfolding of Last Things in the Last Days see these as the literal twelve tribes of

Israel. But the twelve tribes listed here are not identical with the list of tribes in the book of Joshua who settle their Promised Land. Author John includes ten of the twelve tribes, omitting two of the Old Testament twelve and including two not in the original lineup.

Then ten in both listings are Judah, Reuben, Gad, Asher, Naphtali, Manasseh, Simeon, Issachar, Zebulun, and Benjamin. The two tribes John omits are Ephraim and Dan. In their places, John includes Joseph and Levi. Scholars offer assorted conjectures regarding these variations.

We will return to the significance of listing the hundred forty-four thousand shortly as we try to understand the second vision (verses 9-17), involving a much larger group.

In a near replay of the heavenly court scene from chapters 4-5, we once again are *standing before the throne and before the Lamb*. But this time, *a great multitude which no man could number, from every nation, from all tribes and peoples and tongues* is there, dressed in white robes and carrying palm branches in their hands. All these folks are there along with the angels and the elders and the four living creatures who are doing what they do best: *crying out with a loud voice, "Salvation belongs to our God who sits upon the throne, and to the Lamb!"* The heavenly beings fall on their faces before the throne and worship God as they say, *Amen! Blessing and glory and wisdom and thanksgiving and honor and power and might be to our God for ever and ever! Amen.*

One of the twenty-four elders asks John whether he knows who these people in white robes are. John says, in effect, "You'd better tell me." So the elder explains, *"These are they who have come out of the great tribulation; they have washed their robes and made them white in the blood of the Lamb."*

Only in figurative language do you wash garments in blood and have them come out white. But these people came to God through faith in Jesus, the Lamb who was slain.

So Who Are These Two Groups?

In symbolic understanding, the hundred forty-four thousand is the number of Christians on earth, those who have received the seal of God. We've seen many examples of the symbolic number *seven*. Now consider the number *twelve*. Twelve tribes and twelve apostles readily come to mind.

Later in Revelation, we will discover more *twelves*: The heavenly New Jerusalem will have *twelve gates, and at the gates twelve angels, and on the gates the names of the twelve tribes of the sons of Israel . . . And the wall of the city had twelve foundations, and on them the twelve names of the twelve apostles of the Lamb* (21:12-14). Each of the twelve gates is made of one huge pearl (21:21).

In numerical symbolism, when you multiply a number, you intensify its significance. Twelve squared is one hundred forty-four. Multiply that by a thousand, and you have the hundred forty-four thousand. Thus, the perfect number of God's people on earth have received the seal of God on their foreheads.

As for the twelve tribes representing Christians rather than Jews, St. Paul points to the Israel of God (Galatians 6:16), and – as a Jew himself – Paul says "real" Jewishness is inward, spiritual, not literal, a circumcision of the heart rather than the body. In symbolism parallel to cutting away the flesh in the rite for Jewish males, circumcision of the heart means cutting away unclean aspects of the spirit (Romans 2:28-29).

Not everyone is happy with the interpretation of Christians as "spiritual Israel." For those who see Revelation as a road map for the end time, the literal, historical twelve tribes of Israel become extremely significant: Christ on a throne in Jerusalem, ruling over a restored biblical Israel, is central to the theology of many who look for His imminent return to rapture the church out of the world, followed eventually by that earthly reign of Jesus. We will look at this interpretation in some detail later in this study.

The Jehovah's Witnesses church group believes only one hundred forty-four thousand people will get to heaven. Their faithful who go door to door hope to be in that number. If they don't make the cut, they will inherit the earth, and the rest of us will be obliterated. Their projected smallish number in heaven is difficult to reconcile with the countless number of martyrs who enjoy heavenly rest in verses 9-12.

This entire interlude offers assurance to the first century readers for themselves and for their fellow believers who have gone through tribulation. The chapter concludes with a description of that countless number and their blessings as they died in the great tribulation:

"Therefore are they before the throne of God,
and serve him day and night within his temple;
and he who sits upon the throne will shelter them
    with his presence.
They shall hunger no more, neither thirst any more;
the sun shall not strike them, nor any scorching heat.
For the Lamb in the midst of the throne will be their shepherd,
and he will guide them to springs of living water;
and God will wipe away every tear from their eyes" (vv. 15-17).

Finally, after the pause for these visions, the seventh seal will be opened in chapter 8:1, followed by another interlude: a dramatic half hour of silence to create suspense for those viewing the spectacle in heaven's throne room before a new set of visions involving seven trumpets.

Chapters 8-11

Apocalypse In The Modern Sense

We noted earlier in the introduction to this book how the original biblical meaning of *apocalypse* has undergone drastic change. The Greek word simply means *revelation*. That's how the book got its English name. In the Greek New Testament, its name is *Apocalupsis*. The full Greek name is *Apocalupsis Iwannou*, which means *The Apocalypse of John* or *The Revelation of John*. Somewhere along the way, though, *apocalypse* has come to mean *disaster* or *catastrophic destruction*. As we come to the blowing of the seven trumpets in chapters 8-11, we may feel the modern usage of the word is justified because the earth, sea, and sky undergo great devastation. Also, some human beings undergo torture, and others die as God sends preliminary judgment. Even so, Author John uses *apocalypse* only to mean *revelation*. He would not appreciate our twentieth and twenty-first century usage of the word.

The First Four Trumpets

After the half hour of silence, John sees *the seven angels who stand before God*, who are given seven trumpets. These *seven angels who stand before God* are stock characters in Jewish apocalyptic writings (See Tobit 12:15 and 1 Enoch 81:5). Before the seven angels blow their trumpets, yet another angel with an incense pot *is given much incense prayers of all the saints upon the golden altar before the throne*. The prayers and smoke from the incense rise to God. Then the angel replaces the incense with fire and throws the fire to the earth, bringing thunder, voices, lightning, and an earthquake – a preview of judgment to come as the trumpets sound.

Destruction rains down on earth with the sounding of the trumpets, partial rather than complete destruction, mostly coming in thirds, to the earth, sea, rivers, and the sun, moon, and stars:

The first angel's trumpet brings hail and fire, mixed with blood, and a third of the earth and a third of the trees are burnt up, and all green grass is burnt up.

After the second trumpet is blown *something like a great mountain, burning with fire* is thrown into the sea, and there is more destruction by thirds in the sea: a third of the sea became blood, a third of the sea creatures die, and a third of the ships are destroyed.

With the third trumpet, a great blazing star or angel named Wormwood falls from heaven, turning a third of the rivers bitter. Many who drink the water die (the wormwood shrub has a bitter taste).

The fourth blast brings darkness to the day and the night as a third of the sun, moon, and stars are struck.

An eagle in midheaven then proclaims three woes on the earth's residents as the three remaining trumpets are about to blow.

The Fifth And Sixth Trumpets

With the fifth trumpet, another star or angel falls from heaven and is given *the key of the shaft of the bottomless pit.* We will see this bottomless pit again in chapters 11 and 20. When the angel opens the shaft, smoke belches forth like a furnace, darkening the sun and the air. Amid the smoke, a terrifying army rises out of the pit: an army of locusts, like no locusts the world has known:

They look like horses arrayed for battle; on their heads are what looks like crowns of gold; their faces like human faces, their hair like women's hair, their teeth like lions' teeth; their scales like iron breastplates, and noise of their wings like many chariots with horses rushing into battle. Their tails are like scorpions, and the pain they inflict is like a scorpion's sting. Their stings can hurt men for five months. This time limit indicates the pain is not fatal. The locusts even have a king: the angel of the bottomless pit, whose name in Hebrew is Abaddon, and in Greek he is called Apollyon (9:7-11). Both names mean *Destroyer*.

Although the locusts' sting is not fatal, it is so severe that people long for death. The locusts' tails are like serpents, with heads, and by means of them they wound those *who have not the seal of God upon their foreheads* (9:4). Recall the perfect number of people (one hundred forty-four thousand) from the twelve tribes, in chapter 7 who have been sealed. Also, the seals on the foreheads anticipate the contrast with the mark of the beast in chapter 13.

When the locust invasion ends, the first woe is over.

The sixth trumpet calls out a second army – human cavalrymen. The riders' breastplates are the color of fire, sapphire, and sulphur. The horses remind us of the locusts: their heads like lions. Fire and smoke and sulphur issue from the horses' mouths, killing a third of humanity. The horses' tails are like serpents, and the tails have heads with which they can wound.

Those who are not killed by the plagues of fire, sapphire, and sulphur refuse to repent. They have not given up *worshiping demons and idols of gold and silver and bronze and stone and wood, which cannot either see or hear or walk.* These idols call to mind those who burn incense at the Emperor's altar which John warns the churches about in the letters in chapters 2-3. The unrepentant are also guilty of murder, sorceries, immorality, and theft.

This cavalry unit is an impossibly large number: two hundred million men on horseback. Ray Summers estimated this formation would be a mile wide and eighty-five miles long.[14a] We should not equate these troops with a literal, physical army, past or present. Rather, think in figurative terms of God's power against Rome.

Judgment In Hebrew Scripture

Author John finds inspiration in his Hebrew Scripture for some of the descriptions with the trumpets. He may have had in mind several of the plagues depicted in Exodus as judgment on Egypt from God as Moses tried to get Pharaoh to let the Israelites go: The first trumpet brings hail and fire mixed with blood, reminiscent of an Egyptian plague in Exodus 9:18. With the second trumpet, a third of the sea turns to blood, similar to a plague in Exodus 7:19. The fourth trumpet brings darkness, which resembles Exodus 10:21-22. In Exodus 10:4-6, the Egyptians were overrun with locusts, as with the fifth trumpet.

John may also be thinking of the Hebrew prophet Joel who preaches during an infestation of locusts. Joel also likens the locusts to war horses (Joel 2:4-5).

We see God's judgment in each setting: Moses with the plagues, Joel with the locusts, John with the trumpets.

Multifaceted Interlude

Chapter 10 and most of 11 provide an interlude with several distinct scenes between the sounding of the sixth and seventh trumpets.

Seven Thunders

In the first scene, another mighty angel comes down from heaven. He is wrapped in a cloud, a rainbow over his head, his face like the sun, legs like pillars of fire, and a voice like a roaring lion. He has a little scroll in his hand as he stands with his right foot on the sea, the left foot on the land. This stance indicates his message is for the whole world. When this angel speaks, John hears seven thunders. Assuming he is to write another series of sevens, after the fashion of the seven seals and the seven trumpets, he grabs his scroll and reaches for his pen. But a voice from heaven tells John not to write.

What are the seven thunders? Their content and meaning are forever sealed. Perhaps Author John seals the thunders as a tantalizing secret. Perhaps he considers the length of his manuscript and decides not to develop that sevenfold series.

We simply do not know the content, but that does not inhibit people from developing websites to provide many answers, both theological and secular under the title "Seven Thunders":

- The future for America, with prophecy charts
- Ecumenical multi-day spiritual retreats
- A Christian answer to the world's economic problems and unemployment
- Cards to tell your destiny
- A 1957 Swedish film with the tale of British prisoners of war who escape and hide out in German-occupied France

We may not find a more common sense explanation of the sealing of the seven thunders than in the Revelation volume of the 1884 *An American Commentary on the New Testament.* Baptist scholar Justin A. Smith notes: "Questions offer themselves as to the reason of this injunction [not to write about the thunders], as well as the import of the utterances themselves." But Dr. Smith's only explanation is this: "There must have been a purpose in the utterances and a purpose also in the command not to write."[14b]

These interpretations of the seven thunders are an example of how people latch onto one detail in Revelation and run amok with ideas that have no apparent biblical connection.

After the angel seeks to lay the seven thunders to rest, he swears by the eternal creator of all things that the great mystery God had announced to the prophets is about to be fulfilled with the sounding of the seventh trumpet.

In his oath, the angel does not call the name of God. Rather, he swears *by him who lives for ever and ever, who created heaven and what is in it, the earth and what is in it, and the sea and what is in it, that there should be no more delay.* This hesitation to call the Holy Name reminds us of the scene in the heavenly throne room in chapters 4-5: There, God the Father is simply called *him who is seated on the throne.*

The Little Scroll

After the seven thunders are sealed, the voice from heaven speaks again, telling John to take the little scroll from the hand of the angel. When John takes the scroll, the voice tells him to eat it, warning it will taste sweet as honey in John's mouth but will be bitter in his stomach. That word comes true as the angel tells John, *You must again prophesy about many peoples and nations and tongues and kings.* We will hear that bitter message in the second half of Revelation, beginning in chapter 12.

Measuring The Temple

After John eats the little scroll, he is given a measuring rod and told to measure the Temple, but only the inner court. The Temple complex in Jerusalem included a large outer court non-Jews could enter with no problem. John is specifically told not to measure this "court of the Gentiles." The angel explains this prohibition: *for it is given over to the nations, and they will trample over the holy city for forty-two months. And I will grant my two witnesses power to proph-*

esy for one thousand two hundred and sixty days, clothed in sackcloth.

We will look closely at those *two witnesses* shortly. Even though the measuring and the witnesses may seem incidental to some readers, both elements provide rich veins for those who mine every line of Revelation in search of meanings for the end time.

Let's begin the measuring sequence by remembering the historic physical Temple in Jerusalem was destroyed in A. D. 70, so it is in ruins by the time John writes Revelation near the end of the first Christian century. So John is not told to go to Jerusalem with a surveying team.

In the minds of those who look for Jesus to rule from a throne in Jerusalem, this measuring will take place in preparation for the thousand-year reign. Gentiles who did not convert during the Tribulation will have no part in the millennium. These nonbelievers are those who *will trample over the holy city for forty-two months.* That period is three and a half years, half of the anticipated seven years of Tribulation.

NOTE: *See Appendix B for more on The Great Tribulation.*

If you realize Revelation had specific meaning for its original readers, you see the measuring from a different perspective. Measuring the Temple is the means of accounting for the people of God, followers of Lamb who was slain. At this point, there is no need to account for those who persecute the Christian church as they *trample over the holy city for forty-two months.*

That amount of time – *forty-two months*, three and a half years – is half the perpetual *seven*, symbolic of completeness. As a fragment, this number reminds us the trampling on holy things and holy people is not total and absolute. The Christian movement will not be overcome.

The Two Witnesses (11:3-13)

As we go from measuring the Temple and move to the two witnesses, we see the same fragmentary time indications expressed variously: *one thousand two hundred and sixty days*, the same as *forty-two months*; and also *three days and a half*. All three express lack of completeness.

The two witnesses will prophesy for this incomplete period: *And I will grant my two witnesses power to prophesy for one thousand two hundred and sixty days, clothed in sackcloth* (11:2).

We are given no clear identity of the witnesses, but we have hints pointing in two different directions. First (11:4): *These are the two olive trees and the two lampstands which stand before the Lord of the earth*. This seems to be an allusion to two faithful witnesses, Zerubbabel and Joshua, in the prophecy of Zechariah who are called olive trees and lampstands (See Zechariah 4).

On the other hand, Revelation 11:6 suggests Elijah and Moses: *They have power to shut the sky, that no rain may fall during the days of their prophesying, and they have power over the waters to turn them into blood, and to smite the earth with every plague, as often as they desire.* Elijah declared no rain would fall until he commanded it (1 Kings 17:1). And, under Moses's leadership, various plagues fell on Egypt (Exodus, chapters 7-11).

Whoever the two witnesses are, God will preserve them as they bring their message, and God gives them power to overcome their foes (v. 5). But when they finish their testimony, *the beast that ascends from the bottomless pit will make war upon them and conquer them and kill them, and their dead bodies will lie in the street of the great city allegorically called Sodom and Egypt, where their Lord was crucified* (vv. 7-8). To some interpreters, the allegorical reference to Sodom and Egypt suggests Rome, but the reference to *where their Lord was crucified* clearly suggests Jerusalem. *Allegorically* should be our operative word and make us slow to take this passage literally.

When the beast kills the two witnesses, their bodies lie in the street *three days and a half*. This causes widespread rejoicing among *those who dwell on the earth*. This includes *peoples and tribes and tongues and nations* (vv. 9-10). The wider context of the book suggests these who rejoice over the death of the witnesses are the persecutors of the church.

With the symbolic incompleteness of *three and a half*, we see in verse 11: *But after the three and a half days a breath of life from God entered them, and they stood up on their feet, and great fear fell on those who saw them.*

As the two witnesses are slain and brought back to life, the original readers are reminded that torture or even death is not the end for the people of God and their messengers. This is underscored in verse 12: *Then they heard a loud voice from heaven saying to them, "Come up hither!" And in the sight of their foes they went up to heaven in a cloud.*

This final scene in the interlude between the sixth and seventh trumpets, with great and terrifying exhibition of God's power (v. 13): *And at that hour there was a great earthquake, and a tenth of the city fell; seven thousand people were killed in the earthquake, and the rest were terrified and gave glory to the God of heaven.*

People have guessed at the witnesses' identities throughout Christian history. The guessers usually try to connect events in their own current times with specific passages in Revelation. They expect two witnesses to show up in their generation and speak words of faithful witness as history as we know it comes to an end. Here are some of the guesses as to who or what the witnesses are:

- The Old and New Testaments
- Israel and the Christian Church
- Elijah and Moses who will come back at the end time, bear witness, be slain, then be brought back to life, and raptured to heaven
- Men not yet revealed who will witness to the Jews and bring about their conversion as Christ sets up His earthly kingdom in Jerusalem

So who are the two witnesses? Someone observed, "Who they are must not be terribly important, or we would have been told exactly who they are!" Good point.

With all the carnage of the visions throughout chapters 6-11, keep in mind they are visions. They are not records of actual destruction of nature and the slaughter of men and women. Also remember, a chief characteristic of apocalyptic literature is a massive conflict between the forces of good and evil. We have seen many illustrations of that characteristic in these chapters.

With the witnesses' return to heaven, we learn (v. 14), *The second woe has passed; behold, the third woe is soon to come.*

The Seventh Trumpet

At long last, the seventh trumpet sounds, and loud voices in heaven declare God has triumphed over the forces of evil. We are only halfway through Revelation, so this announcement may seem premature. And, indeed, the battle between the forces of good and evil is only about to unfold as the Lamb who was slain continues to reveal the full story to John and others gathered in the viewing room of the throne room of heaven. But, as we've already noted, we were told from the get-go, the Lamb will win this titanic struggle which seems without end.

George Frederick Handel quotes the triumphant words of those heavenly voices in his great "Hallelujah" chorus from *Messiah*: "The kingdom of the world is become the kingdom of our Lord and of his Christ, and he shall reign for ever and ever."

We are back in the throne room where the vision began in chapter 4-5. Once again, the *twenty-four elders* we met earlier lead in praise and worship of God (11:16-19):

And the twenty-four elders who sit on their thrones before God fell on their faces and worshiped God, saying, "We give thanks to thee, Lord God Almighty, who art and who wast, that thou hast taken thy great power and begun to reign. The nations raged, but thy wrath came, and the time for the dead to be judged, for rewarding thy servants, the prophets and saints, and those who fear thy name, both small and great, and for destroying the destroyers of the earth."

Then God's temple in heaven was opened, and the ark of his covenant was seen within his temple; and there were flashes of lightning, voices, peals of thunder, an earthquake, and heavy hail.

The Solid Rock

Echoing the First Century Christians' confidence in the ultimate triumph of Christ, Edward Mote, a nineteenth century British Baptist pastor and hymn writer, wrote "The Solid Rock":

*My hope is built on nothing less
Than Jesus' blood and righteous;
No merit of my own I claim
But wholly lean on Jesus' name.*

*When darkness veils his lovely face,
I rest on his unchanging grace;
In every high and story gale
My anchor holds within the veil.*

*His oath, his covenant, his blood,
Sustain me in the raging flood;
When all supports are washed away,
He then is all my hope and stay.*

*When he shall come with trumpet sound,
Oh, may I then in him be found,
Clothed in his righteousness alone,
Redeemed to stand before the throne!*

*On Christ, the solid rock, I stand;
All other ground is sinking sand.*[15]

5 – Revelation, Chapters 12-13: The Woman Clad in the Sun, the Dragon, and the Two Beasts

Chapter 12: The Woman and the Dragon

The Christmas Story Writ Large

When we think of the biblical story of Christmas, we probably think of the shepherds and the angels in Luke or the Wise Men in Matthew. But several other books of the Bible, including Revelation, tell of the birth of Jesus:

The opening verses of the Gospel of John describe Jesus as the eternal Word, who was one with God from the beginning. Then, in John's version of Christmas, he says, *And the Word became flesh and dwelt among us, full of grace and truth; we have beheld his glory, glory as of the only Son from the Father* (John 1:14).

Among the four Gospels, Mark alone makes no mention of Jesus's birth or childhood. By the ninth verse, Jesus is a grown man who gets baptized.

In Galatians, St. Paul says Jesus was born according to God's divine timetable in order for the human race to become God's adopted children: *But when the time had fully come, God sent forth his Son, born of woman, born under the law, to redeem those who were under the law, so that we might receive adoption as sons* (Galatians 4:4-5).

Philippians says Jesus was in the very form of God, but He gave up all His heavenly perks and took on the form of a man, willingly dying on the cross for the human race:

Have this mind among yourselves, which is yours in Christ Jesus, who, though he was in the form of God, did not count equality with God a thing to be grasped, but emptied himself, taking the form of a servant, being born in the likeness of men. And being found in human form he humbled himself and became obedient unto death, even death on a cross (Philippians 2:5-9).

An Epic Event In Revelation

As you've learned to expect by now, when it comes to Revelation, the birth of Jesus is described in larger-than-life terms, rather than Luke's straightforward description: *And she gave birth to her first-born son and wrapped him in swaddling cloths, and laid him in a manger, because there was no place for them in the inn* (Luke 2:7).

The dramatic description of Jesus's birth in chapter 12 of Revelation deserves the overworked word *epic*. This birth is not hidden away in a smelly cow stall behind a small hotel. Instead, Author John says it is a *portent* (which means an event drawing attention to itself), setting off a battle with a red dragon. Presence of the dragon – identified in verse 9 as *that ancient serpent* [recalling the tempter in Genesis 3 in the form of a serpent], *who is called the Devil and Satan, the deceiver of the whole world* – indicates the beginning of a war that will extend through chapter 20:

And a great portent appeared in heaven, a woman clothed with the sun, with the moon under her feet, and on her head a crown of twelve stars; she was with child and she cried out in her pangs of birth, in anguish for delivery (vv. 1-2).

This description is such a far cry from the little town of Bethlehem that we may not see the connection with Jesus at first. But the first Christian readers would see a messianic reference in verse 5: *she brought forth a male child, one who is to rule all the nations with a rod of iron*. The rod of iron is mentioned in Psalm 2, generally interpreted as messianic.

Still the woman in verse 1 bears little resemblance to Mary: *a woman clothed with the sun, with the moon under her feet, and on her head a crown of twelve stars.*

And probably she is not Mary. The exalted woman, clothed in splendor and majesty, has also been identified as the historic nation of Israel, whose prophets foretold the coming Messiah; the Jews at the time of Jesus's birth; and generally the people of God, people of faith. Properly understood, the woman is not the Church because Jesus gave birth to the Church rather than the other way around.

As the woman is in the travail of labor, the red dragon appears *before the woman who was about to bear a child, that he might devour her child when she brought it forth.* He also is a *portent*, a sight to behold, *with seven heads and ten horns, and seven diadems upon his heads* (vv. 3-4). With both seven and ten symbolizing power, the dragon's heads and horns and crowns all point to his power and authority over the forces of evil.

Need we say again, all this is figurative language? The dragon is so big and lumbering, when he swishes his tail, he knocks a third of the stars out of the sky, and they fall to earth (v. 4). All this is happening in the heavenly realms.

When the child is born, the woman flees to a place of safety God has prepared in the wilderness. We need not worry about the incongruity of language as the wilderness seems to be in heaven. She and the child are there twelve hundred sixty days (or three and a half years), the incomplete time we noticed in chapter 11 with the two witnesses.

Led by Michael, the angels of heaven rally against the red dragon as he tries to destroy the child. Michael is an angelic figure from the book of Daniel as well as Jewish books that did not find acceptance as Holy Scripture. The angels throw the dragon down to earth. Again, we see the figurative or spiritual nature of this battle: No weapons are listed, and no one is killed. But the war moves to earth, where it will continue in the coming chapters (vv. 7-9).

A loud voice in heaven declares the salvation and power of the kingdom of God and the authority of Christ in the defeat of the Devil, here called *the accuser* of humanity. Heaven rejoices, but there is woe on earth and in the sea: The Devil has landed with a vengeance because he knows his time is short (v. 10-12), another reminder of the ultimate triumph of God and the Lamb.

On earth, the dragon renews his pursuit of the woman, whose child, meantime, has been taken up to heaven. We are not looking at literal calendar time here. Though it may seem the child has just been born, this reference to his being taken into heaven probably fast forwards to His ascension. The woman is given wings of a great eagle so she can fly away to the safety of the wilderness where she is nourished for three and a half times, that same indefinite period we have seen earlier. The dragon then spews a river out of his mouth in his effort to sweep the woman away in the flood. But earth itself takes on anthropomorphic qualities, opening its mouth and swallowing the river (vv. 13-16).

Angry because the woman has escaped, the dragon goes off *to make war on the rest of her offspring, on those who keep the commandments of God and bear testimony to Jesus.* These are the faithful, who refuse to worship the emperor, choosing instead to *bear testimony to Jesus.* At that point, then, the dragon stands on the sand of the sea (v. 17).

Chapters 13: The Beasts of Revelation

Do you remember Amy from the opening page of this book?

In Amy's adult Sunday school class, when the teacher distributed a list of well-known sayings, Amy insisted "Cleanliness is next to godliness" from the list was in the Bible, although it was said by Susanna Wesley, the mother of John and Charles Wesley, the founders of the Methodist denomination.

The teacher loaned Amy a concordance (a book that locates words and phrases in the Bible), and asked Amy to bring a report to class next Sunday. When the teacher asked Amy whether she found "Cleanliness is next to godliness" in the Bible, Amy declared, "It's in *my* Bible. I *wrote* it in."

Amy has many kinfolks who interpret Revelation. They write in concepts John did not include. We need to keep Amy and company in mind, especially as we try to understand chapter 13 and chapter 19. Two factors seem to cause people to start writing things in: (1) They overlook the historical setting of Revelation, and (2) they give literal interpretations to passages which almost certainly are intended to be read figuratively.

Perhaps we cannot point out too often: the original readers of Revelation were under pressure to worship the Roman emperor, and descriptions of war and strife are veiled references to persecution these early Christians were facing when they refused to burn incense at Caesar's altar. This should cause Amy and others to put away their writing implements and settle for what is actually there.

The Great Beast

Chapter 13 tells of two beasts whom we will designate here as the great beast and the lesser beast. The first verse gives this description of the great beast:

And I saw a beast rising out of the sea, with ten horns and seven heads, with ten diadems upon its horns and a blasphemous name upon its heads.

This great beast sounds like something out of a horror story, not something to be taken literally. And that's probably how the uninitiated would read it if the scroll of Revelation fell into their hands.

The seven-headed monstrosity is a coded reference to the Roman government. The seven heads are a series of Roman emperors who have tortured Christians in that first Christian century. His rising out of the sea suggests he comes from far away – Rome, for example.

Notice two numbers: *Ten* and *seven* both suggest completeness. So the seven-headed beast represents a thorough-going number of emperors who have plagued the church. A horn is a symbol of power, so this beast's ten horns show he is completely in control, humanly speaking.

In addition to the crowns, the great beast wears *a blasphemous name upon its heads*. Various Roman emperors called themselves divine and wore titles such as *Son of God, Savior,* and *Lord.* Some wore these titles lightly, but others took their godhood quite seriously and had people put to death who refused to worship them. Nero is reported to have impaled Christians on stakes and set them on fire as torches in the imperial gardens.

Verse 2 indicates the ferocity of the great beast:

And the beast that I saw was like a leopard, its feet were like a bear's, and its mouth was like a lion's mouth. And to it the dragon gave his power and his throne and great authority.

Author John borrows from the Old Testament book of Daniel (7:2-7) which presents four separate beasts, a lion, a bear, a leopard, and a fourth one identified only as the most ferocious of all, *terrible and dreadful and exceedingly strong.* John combines all these into one.

John says the dragon gave the beast his power, throne, and great authority. In 12:9, the dragon is identified as the serpent, the Devil and Satan and the great deceiver. So John is saying the Roman Empire, in its attacks on Christians, is of the devil.

The beast strongly resembles the dragon: Each has seven heads and ten horns, with crowns on the horns. The dragon is more powerful, as seen in his delegating power to the beast. You can often tell the family a child is from because the child looks so much like the parent. So we might think of the beast as like his father, the Devil.

As you read verse 3, keep in mind, the beast with seven heads represents a series of emperors who torture the Christians:

One of its heads seemed to have a mortal wound, but its mortal wound was healed, and the whole earth followed the beast with wonder.

A popular legend said Nero had come back to life in the person of the later emperor, Domitian. So Nero is represented here as the head that seemed dead but came back to life.

Verses 3-4 describe the great beast's wide following: *and the whole earth followed the beast with wonder. Men worshiped the dragon, for he had given his authority to the beast, and they worshiped the beast, saying, "Who is like the beast, and who can fight against it?"*

Verses 5-6 expand on the great beast's blasphemy:

And the beast was given a mouth uttering haughty and blasphemous words, and it was allowed to exercise authority for forty-two months; it opened its mouth to utter blasphemies against God, blaspheming his name and his dwelling, that is, those who dwell in heaven.

Notice, the great beast *was allowed to exercise authority for forty-two months.* He did not have ultimate power on his own. God *allowed* the beast to exercise his power – for a time. Also notice the numbering. Seven representing completeness, *Forty-two months* is three and a half years. We noted this incomplete number in chapters 11-12. The beast does not have complete authority. This is a word of hope for the churches: The power of Rome will not last.

In real time, John does not live to see the day when Rome ceases to vex the church. That won't end till more than two centuries later when Emperor Constantine becomes a convert and makes Christianity the official religion of the empire. As God counts time, two centuries is brief. But the empire's power in John's time is described further in verses 7-8:

Also it was allowed to make war on the saints and to conquer them. And authority was given it over every tribe and people and tongue and nation, and all who dwell on earth will worship it, every one whose name has not been written before the foundation of the world in the book of life of the Lamb that was slain.

The only people who don't worship the great beast are those whose names are written in *the book of life of the Lamb that was slain.* That is, only faithful Christians refrain from emperor worship.

With pressure mounting to worship the emperor, verses 9-10 are a call to faithful endurance.

If any one has an ear, let him hear: This echoes what Christ said to each of the seven churches back in chapters 2-3. This is what they need to hear in the present moment:

If any one is to be taken captive, to captivity he goes.

This quotation from Jeremiah15:2 acknowledges the power of the secular ruler. If you are taken prisoner, there's no point trying to resist. In the present situation, the Roman empire is too strong.

Then John uses another quotation, this one from Jesus as He is arrested (Matthew 26:52):

[I]*f any one slays with the sword, with the sword must he be slain.*

At the arrest, when Peter uses his sword to cut off a servant's ear, Jesus tells him to put away the sword. Consider two points about not taking up the sword: (1) In Peter's immediate situation, any effort to keep the Roman soldiers from taking Jesus prisoner could be suicidal. And (2), taking the longer look, the church should remember its power is not in the literal metallic sword. The church should not rely on military power to accomplish its purpose. With the strong militaristic outlook of many Christians in our own time, we forget most Christians were pacifists until Constantine embraced the church in A. D. 312. John's original readers could not in conscience take up arms in behalf of the pagan government.

These warnings ends in verse 10 with a specific call to remain faithful:

Here is a call for the endurance and faith of the saints.

The Lesser Beast

We hear so much about the beast of Revelation, we may think there is only *one* beast, but a second beast shows up in verse 11: *Then I saw another beast which rose out of the earth; it had two horns like a lamb and it spoke like a dragon.*

Notice the difference between the two beasts. Instead of ten horns, this beast has only two horns. No multiple heads, no crowns.

Two horns like a lamb call to mind that Jesus frequently is referred to in Revelation as the Lamb Who was slain. So we have here a beast in Lamb's clothing. It looks like a lamb, but it speaks like a dragon. It masquerades to look like Jesus, but in reality it is of the Devil.

The great beast came out of the sea from far away. The lesser beast *rose out of the earth*. He is the local representative of the emperor, enforcing worship at the emperor's altar. In verse 12, he carries the authority of Rome, forcing the local inhabitants to worship the Big Guy:

It exercises all the authority of the first beast in its presence, and makes the earth and its inhabitants worship the first beast, whose mortal wound was healed.

In verses 13-14, our second beast, who looks like Christ but speaks for the devil, is a wonder worker, *even making fire come down from heaven to earth in the sight of men*, after the fashion of Elijah the ancient prophet (2 Kings 1:10). This lesser beast deceives people, calling on them to *make an image for the beast which was wounded by the sword and yet lived.* This again reflects the tradition of *Nero redivivus* (Nero come back to life).

Verse 15 indicates this flashy junior grade beast is a ventriloquist: *it was allowed to give breath to the image of the beast so that the image of the beast should even speak.*

The latter part of verse 15 refers to the slaughter of those who refuse to worship the image of the emperor: The lesser beast would *cause those who would not worship the image of the beast to be slain.*

The Mark Of The Beast

Then in verses 16-18, we come to the famous or infamous mark of the beast which is administered by the local religious leaders who enforce emperor worship:

Also it causes all, both small and great, both rich and poor, both free and slave, to be marked on the right hand or the forehead, so that no one can buy or sell unless he has the mark, that is, the name of the beast or the number of its name. This calls for wisdom: let him who has understanding reckon the number of the beast, for it is a human number, its number is six hundred and sixty-six.

Apparently, there was some kind of actual marking on the *right hand or the forehead* a person was required to have in order to buy or sell. This would have been similar to brands placed on runaway slaves who came back to their owners; or a tattoo a soldier often voluntarily wore with the name of his general. A more recent example of a literal mark was in World War Two when Nazis placed a physical means of identifying Jews to set them off. At first, while they still were in their hometowns, Jews were forced to pin yellow stars to their outer garments. Later, they received permanently tattooed numbers on their bodies.

The mark of the beast in Revelation was identification of those who were in good standing with the emperor because they had burned incense. Christians who refused and did not have the mark were discriminated against in various ways – being unable to buy food or other necessities, fined, exiled, imprisoned, or put to death.

John concludes his discussion of the mark of the beast this way:

This calls for wisdom: let him who has understanding reckon the number of the beast, for it is a human number, its number is six hundred and sixty-six.

He calls on fellow Christians to exercise wisdom in order to understand what he is saying about the mark of the beast. The mark is a number, *a human number* – that is, the number is related to a person. And the number is 666 in most ancient manuscripts of Revelation. However, some manuscripts have the number as 616.

Ancient cultures often gave numerical value to letters of the alphabet. In modern usage, the simplest in English would make A equal 1, B equal 2, C equal 3, and so on with Z equalling 26. But there have been many numbering systems throughout history. Bible scholars have found numbers using Hebrew or Greek or Latin letters to make the name and title *Nero Caesar* equal 666, reflecting the tradition of Nero come back to life in Domitian. Another numbering scheme finds *Nero Caesar* adding up to 616. So scholars have pointed to both 666 and 616 as indicators of Nero as the beast.

Before we finish with the mark of the beast, we will remind ourselves of another kind of marking in Revelation.

Modern Misinterpretations

Now, we've seen the straightforward explanation of what the mark of the beast meant in the first century. It was an identifying mark worn by people who burned incense at the altar to Caesar. But you may be aware of all sorts of fantastic interpretations floating around out there on radio and TV and books such as the *Left Behind* series.

Men with good intentions publish books to spell out all that's going to happen at the end of time. They get carried away and follow their good intentions into Fantasy Land.

These date-setters are Amy's cousins, making connections the Bible never makes. For example, they call the great beast in Revelation the Antichrist. In a separate section, we will see what the Bible does and does not say about the Antichrist (see pages 78-86). People make this unbiblical connection because they don't believe Revelation was written primarily for people in the first Christian century. They ignore the simple explanation about the coded message to Christians who suffered threats of death for refusing to worship Caesar as god.

To connect the mark of the beast with their own generation, people have assigned numerical values to letters in the names Adolph Hitler and the Roman Catholic Pope and come up with 666.

When President Franklin Roosevelt back in the 1930s got Congress to pass the Social Security Act, some people were sure their Social Security number was the mark of the beast. More recently, bar codes have been identified as the mark.

Regarding bar codes, a youth-oriented workbook from a religious publisher included a graphic illustration: There's a full-page drawing of a man, sitting with his elbows on a desk and his chin resting on his hands. He is branded *both* on his right hand and on the forehead. On his right hand, 666 is written large. Then, on the man's forehead, there's a bar code, like the one the clerk at the grocery store uses to ring up the cost of a loaf of bread or a bottle of catsup. And under the bar code, 666 again, this time in small type.[16]

In recent years, telephone companies have had blowback when they assigned 666 as prefixes to phone numbers. In 2008, residents of the small town of Reeves, Louisiana, were allowed to change their prefixes from the number they considered to be of the Devil. The mayor of Reeves was quoted as saying the phone company's decision was "divine intervention."[17]

Students and administrators at the small non-denominational Kentucky Mountain Bible College near Lexington objected when the school was assigned the 666 prefix. One student said she was shocked when she heard the news. A vice president said the number was not a problem "in the secular world," but it was to them. The phone company changed the college's prefix.[17a]

I personally learned of a similar concern several years ago in a suburb of Waco, Texas, when residents received the dread prefix. That problem also was resolved by the phone company.

Darby-Scofield System

To get fuller perspective on the viewpoint reflected under the previous heading, we need to look briefly at a widely used approach to interpreting the end times. Those who read Revelation primarily for clues to the end of the world do not all read it the same way. But there are at least seven phases the futurists seem to agree on, as outlined initially in the mid-eighteen hundreds by an Anglo-Irish evangelist named John Nelson Darby. His approach to *eschatology* (eschaton = Greek word for *end times*) was popularized in the United States by C. I. Scofield through his Scofield Reference Bible, first published in 1909.[18]

The Rapture – Christ will usher in what we might call "the beginning of the end" as He appears in the sky, rapturing His disciples, that is, catching them up to meet Him in the air and taking them to heaven to escape the next phase.

The Tribulation Period – A seven-year period will follow the Rapture, with severe persecution for those who are "left behind."

[One point of disagreement is the timeframe for the the Rapture and the Tribulation, with at least three prefixes for Tribulation: pre-trib, post-trib, and mid-trib. The church will be raptured before the Tribulation, after the Tribulation, or in the midst of the Tribulation, respectively.]

The Antichrist – This lawless figure will set himself up as God, and bring great persecution as he seeks world domination. This rivalry will culminate with battle at Armageddon (See the next section).

The Battle of Armageddon – In great literal blood-and-guts warfare in the area of Megiddo , Christ will triumph over the forces of evil. He will cast the beast and false prophet into the lake of fire.

The Millennium – After the battle at Armageddon, Christ will rule for a millennium (a thousand years) from a restored throne in Jerusalem. The Devil will be chained during the millennium. Afterward, he will be released to do evil for a season. But fire from heaven will overcome his forces. Then he will be thrown into the lake of fire along with the beast and false prophet.

The Final Judgment – All souls on earth will be judged and assigned eternally to live with God or burn in hell. [Some see two or more judgments, others see only one judgment.]

The New Heaven and New Earth – God will make all things new.

The Mark Of The Living God

Revelation has another mark that gets lost in the hype over the mark of the beast. In chapter 7, God's people are given seals on their foreheads, a mark of God's protection. Those who worship the emperor receive his mark, but God's people receive God's seal.

Then I saw another angel ascend from the rising of the sun, with the seal of the living God, and he called with a loud voice to the four angels who had been given power to harm earth and sea, saying, "Do not harm the earth or the sea or the trees, till we have sealed the servants of our God upon their foreheads" (7:2-3).

In verse 4, a perfect number of God's people receive the seal, a hundred forty-four thousand from every tribe of the sons of Israel, a symbol of the church as the new Israel.

More directly to the point, in 14:1-3 – immediately following the beast's mark here in chapter 13 – the same symbolism appears again, in striking contrast with the beast's marking:

Then I looked, and lo, on Mount Zion stood the Lamb, and with him a hundred and forty-four thousand who had his name and his Father's name written on their foreheads. And I heard a voice from heaven like the sound of many waters and like the sound of loud thunder; the voice I heard was like the sound of harpers playing on their harps, and they sing a new song before the throne and before the four living creatures and before the elders. No one could learn that song except the hundred and forty-four thousand who had been redeemed from the earth.

A Word Of Summary

Lots of people think the beast is a man who will control the world prior to Christ's return. But, remember, Revelation was written to console Christians in the first century who were facing extreme persecution. The message was in a code church folks would understand but their torturers in the Roman government likely would NOT understand.

Here, then, is the lesson for us in the Twenty-First Century regarding the beast and his mark. We shouldn't worry about some big bugaboo with seven heads and ten horns plastering some kind of a mark on people's foreheads or hands. Indeed, we need not think in literal terms about marks on the foreheads of God's Elect or on the foreheads of those who bow at Caesar's altar. Rather, God has marked people He loves, people who live in His care and commit themselves to Him.

A Mighty Fortress Is Our God

Perhaps reflecting biblical times, Europeans in the sixteenth century believed veritable armies of unseen forces, good and evil, hovered all around, ready to lift them up or tear them down. In that environment, the Devil is reported to have been so real to Protestant Reformer Martin Luther that he threw an ink well at the looming presence he felt was in the room with him.

Luther's hymn of the Reformation reflects the reality of the presence of evil as a threat to spiritual welfare but also expresses confidence in the triumph of God through Christ. Two sets of texts follow. The first version is found in various Protestant hymnals. The second text, probably truer to Luther's own words, was found online at www.lutheran-hymnal.com/lyrics/tlh262.htm.

Ecumenical Text
A mighty fortress is our God, a bulwark never failing;
Our helper He, amid the flood of mortal ills prevailing:
For still our ancient foe doth seek to work us woe;
His craft and power are great, and, armed with cruel hate,
On earth is not his equal.

Did we in our own strength confide, our striving would be losing;
Were not the right Man on our side, the Man of God's
own choosing:
Dost ask who that may be? Christ Jesus, it is He;
Lord Sabaoth, His Name, from age to age the same,
And He must win the battle.

And though this world, with devils filled, should threaten
to undo us,
We will not fear, for God hath willed His truth to triumph
through us:
The Prince of Darkness grim, we tremble not for him;
His rage we can endure, for lo, his doom is sure,
One little word shall fell him.

That word above all earthly powers, no thanks to them, abideth;
   The Spirit and the gifts are ours through Him Who with us sideth:
   Let goods and kindred go, this mortal life also;
   The body they may kill: God's truth abideth still,
   His kingdom is forever.[19]

<u>Lutheran Text</u>
Composite Translation from the Pennsylvania Lutheran
CHURCH BOOK of 1868

A mighty Fortress is our God,
A trusty Shield and Weapon;
He helps us free from every need
That hath us now o'ertaken.
The old evil Foe
Now means deadly woe;
Deep guile and great might
Are his dread arms in fight;
On Earth is not his equal.

With might of ours can naught be done,
Soon were our loss effected;
But for us fights the Valiant One,
Whom God Himself elected.
Ask ye, Who is this?
Jesus Christ it is.
Of Sabaoth Lord,
And there's none other God;
He holds the field forever.

Though devils all the world should fill,
All eager to devour us.
We tremble not, we fear no ill,
They shall not overpower us.
This world's prince may still

Scowl fierce as he will,
He can harm us none,
He's judged; the deed is done;
One little word can fell him.

The Word they still shall let remain
Nor any thanks have for it;
He's by our side upon the plain
With His good gifts and Spirit.
And take they our life,
Goods, fame, child and wife,
Let these all be gone,
They yet have nothing won;
The Kingdom our remaineth.[20]

The Antichrist

To get right to the point, Antichrist is not in Revelation. If you find Antichrist in Revelation, you join Amy's Army and *write* him in.

Get a concordance. The venerable *Strong's Exhaustive Concordance* traces every word in the King James Version, including *and, are, but, for, in, of, the, to,* and so on. *Strong's* cites *antichrist* and *antichrists* a total of five times in the whole Bible. Five times. Not one of the five is in Revelation. Four are in First John, the fifth in Second John. Those five references, with their contexts, follow. For convenience of identification, ANTICHRIST is in all caps in the passages which follow.

Read these passages closely. There is no mention of, no connection with, the Rapture, the Tribulation, the Mark of the Beast, the Battle of Armageddon, or the Millennium:

1 John 2:18-22

[18] Children, it is the last hour; and as you have heard that ANTICHRIST is coming, so now many ANTICHRISTS have come; therefore we know that it is the last hour. [19] They went out from us, but they were not of us; for if they had been of us, they would have continued with us; but they went out, that it might be plain that they all are not of us. [20] But you have been anointed by the Holy One, and you all know. [21] I write to you, not because you do not know the truth, but because you know it, and know that no lie is of the truth. [22] Who is the liar but he who denies that Jesus is the Christ? This is the ANTICHRIST, he

who denies the Father and the Son.

Two very interesting things about verse 18:

First, the writer says twice: *it is the last hour.*

Keep in mind, writing nearly two thousand years ago, the writer thought *he* was living in *the last hour.* He says that twice in verse 18.

A second fascinating thing in verse 18:

Sermons on the end time frequently depict *antichrist* as one horrible wooly booger, who will wreak havoc just before Christ comes back to set up an earthly throne in Jerusalem. But verse 18 says *many antichrists have* [already] *come.*

In verse 22, John tells who *the antichrist* is:

Who is the liar but he who denies that Jesus is the Christ? This is the ANTICHRIST, he who denies the Father and the Son.

The word *Christ* is a *title*, recognizing the man Jesus as the Promised Messiah. *Messiah* is the Hebrew word which means *God's Anointed One. Christ* is simply the Greek for that same title: *God's Anointed One.*

So, plainly and simply, *antichrists* are people who deny Jesus is truly the Christ, the Messiah, God's Anointed One. Some people in the early church were among the deniers. *Anti* means *against.* They were *against* Christ, so they were *anti*-christs.

Verse 19 says these folks left the church because they were never true believers: *They went out from us, but they were not of us.*

Within the Christian Church, it is heresy to deny Jesus is the Promised Messiah whose coming fulfilled Old Testament prophecies. As bad as that is theologically, it has no biblical relation to the fictional world ruler coming at the end of time as we know it.

1 John 4:2-4

[2] *By this you know the Spirit of God: every spirit which confesses that Jesus Christ has come in the flesh is of God,* [3] *and every spirit which does not confess Jesus is not of God. This is the spirit of ANTICHRIST, of which you heard that it was coming, and now it is in the world already.* [4] *Little children, you are of God, and have overcome them; for he who is in you is greater than he who is in the world.*

Early heresies, such as docetism, denied Jesus was really a man: He was a demigod posing as a human. Other heresies said He was a man and nothing more. The final *antichrist* verse highlights such heresies:

2 John 7

For many deceivers have gone out into the world, men who will not acknowledge the coming of Jesus Christ in the flesh; such a one is the deceiver and the ANTICHRIST.

They had been church members, but when they started saying Jesus was not really Christ in the flesh, they left the church. Or perhaps the church left them. John calls them *antichrists*.

Then, verses 8-9 again offer a word of warning and an encouraging word:

The warning: *Look to yourselves, that you may not lose what you have worked for, but may win a full reward. Any one who goes ahead and does not abide in the doctrine of Christ does not have God.* In other words, don't YOU be *antichrists*.

Then the encouragement: *[H]e who abides in the doctrine has both the Father and the Son.*

Now, in these three passages, you've read everything the Bible says about *antichrist*. If you equate *antichrist* with the great beast of Revelation, you are writing that into your Bible.

ONE GIANT LEAP

Astronaut Neil Armstrong described his first step as the first man on the moon as "one giant leap for mankind." With apologies to Major General Armstrong, those who link the *antichrists* of First and Second John with the beast of Revelation are taking one giant leap into fiction. Yet, this is a common practice among those with elaborate end-time scenarios.

In the *Left Behind* books, for example, *antichrist* is a man who uses his pleasing personality to become the secretary general of the United Nations Organization as the first step toward heading a world government.

An Internet site lists twelve signs of the end of the world, including the coming of the antichrist. In this scenario, antichrist's arrival will be preceded by deceivers in the name of Christ; wars and rumors of wars; famines, pestilences, and earthquakes; true Christians being hated and killed; false prophets; gospel preached throughout the world; and Jews becoming Christians. Antichrist will persecute the true servants of Christ, and the Temple in Jerusalem will be rebuilt so he can be enthroned there in the place of Christ.[21] To make its point about antichrist, this site lists many Bible references, but none from First or Second John, the only passages that mention *antichrists*.

In another Internet article, "Why the Antichrist Must Come Soon," David J. Stewart says God is angry with America because of abortion, feminism, homosexual marriage, demonic influences in movies and music, and millions of people on welfare. When the nation collapses, antichrist will unite America as "a Godless Global Totalitarian Communist Police State!"[22]

The *antichrist* and the great beast in Revelation also are often linked as an unholy trinity along with an evil person in Second Thessalonians, chapter 2. Various translations identify this third man as the son of perdition, son of destruction, man of sin, man of rebellion, champion of wickedness, and a Wicked One destined for hell. This man is described as one who *takes his seat in the temple of God, proclaiming himself to be God* (2 Thessalonians 2:4). Thus, he and Revelation's great beast have much in common with each other but no biblical connection with the *antichrists* of the Johannine letters.

HOW DID WE GET FROM THERE TO HERE?

We need to ask, How did we get from *there* to *here*? How did we go from *antichrist* as religious heretic to the elaborate claims in churches and on radio, TV, and movies that *antichrist* is the beast?

Jewish tradition includes the idea of a powerful figure who will oppose the Messiah, and the beast of Revelation seems to be related to that general expectation. But, again, it seems a stretch to go from the heretics of the Johannine letters to Revelation's arch fiend, the seven-headed beast. Again, in the Christian Scripture, the antichrist appears only in the letters of John and not in Revelation.

This transfer can be traced at least to the second century, some writings no more than two or three generations after Revelation and the Johannine letters were written. Church leaders in the period following the writings in the New Testament are known as Early Church Fathers. Here are what some of the Fathers wrote:

Polycarp of Smyrna's "Letter to the Philadelphians" in A. D. 135 is thoroughly biblical, a veritable paraphrase of First John. By contrast, Irenaeus approximately half a century later (A. D. 189), claims Antichrist "is anxious to be adored as God." A few years later (A. D. 200), Hippolytus writes of Antichrist as an impersonator of Christ. A decade later, Tertullian (A. D. 210) says Antichrist is the son of perdition in Second Thessalonians. By A. D. 253, Antichrist is a man of violence, according to Cyprian of Carthage.

And on we could go through the early Christian centuries.[23] Our concern here is the biblical picture, but it may be helpful to see how the idea grew after Revelation was written.

Historian and theologian Richard Kyle traces common use of this unbiblical linkage through a millennium of more recent church history. Dr. Kyle cites a monk named Adso who in A. D. 950 predicted the Antichrist would be born in Babylon of the Jewish tribe of Dan. He would perform miracles and claim to be God. He would reign three and a half years, the incomplete timeframe we have noted at several points in Revelation. End-timers take this literally, with the reign of Antichrist occurring during the last half of the Great Tribulation they say will follow the Rapture and precede the Battle of Armageddon.

The title of Kyle's book, *The Last Days Are Here Again, A History of the End Times*, points to the irony of repeated efforts to set dates and map out details for Christ's return.

Troubled times have a special way of getting people to fear the end. This fear finds expression in the desire to be delivered. Things look so bad that some people feel the only way out of this time of difficulty is for Christ to come back and save us from the horrible mess we're in. Kyle documents recurring expectations:

As famine and plague struck Italy in the mid-thirteenth century, groups of men and boys wandered around the country, wailing and beating themselves with iron-spiked leather whips. Many of them expected the end to come in A. D. 1260.[24] When the Black Plague struck about a century later, in 1347, many in Europe saw this as divine punishment, with the end in sight.[25]

During the thirteenth and fourteenth centuries in Europe, because of generally difficult living conditions and the feeling that there was no escape, nearly a dozen different dates were set for the coming of the Antichrist.[26]

From the sixteenth through the eighteenth centuries, the end time was associated with an earthquake in Lisbon, Portugal, and the political upheaval of the

French Revolution. Such learnéd men as the scientist Isaac Newton in the seventeenth century were caught up in this eschatological expectation and tried to figure out when the end would come.[27]

Preachers often latch on to major wars as sure signs the Lord is coming back. Some actually urge American presidents to escalate the wars as a way to hasten the Lord's return. This happened in World War One and is happening with current unrest in the Middle East.

CONCLUDING THOUGHTS

After all these examples from church history, we still have not answered the question of when and how the transformation of *antichrist* began, from heretic to harrower of the church. But this linkage continues in the minds of those who seem certain the end time is right around the corner.

In his 1957 book, *Interpreting Revelation*, Merrill C. Tenney declared Revelation "unmistakably" predicts Christ will lead "a new world order" after the overthrow of a "vast system ruled by an antichrist."[28] He dedicated the book to his two sons "who may live to see the Apocalypse fulfilled." Dr. Tenney did not give his sons' ages, but now they would be at least around sixty years old. Perhaps they share the hope of their father that they will "see the Apocalypse fulfilled."

A newer book, *Living with the End in Sight*, by Kendell Easley in 2000, cites "raw power embodied in the Antichrist," equating Antichrist with the great beast.[29]

Other books, rolling off the press or available through Kindle, doubtlessly will continue this unbiblical linkage of heretics in the letters of John with Revelation's great beast.

Against this background, we do well to remember, the total *antichrist* discussion in First and Second John (and thus in the whole Bible) is an alert and an exhortation for First Century Christians:

Beware of, and do not tolerate, those who deny the central Christian teaching of Jesus as the revelation of God in human form. They are anti-christ. The larger context of First John is a call to love God and love each other and claim forgiveness of sin through Jesus Christ.

6– Revelation, Chapters 14-16: Two Series of Three Angels, Seven Bowls of Wrath, and Preparation for Armageddon

Mine eyes have seen the glory of the coming of the Lord. He is trampling out the *wine press*, where the grapes of wrath are stored...[30]

Julia Ward Howe's original version of the first stanza of "The Battle Hymn of the Republic" in 1861 used the words *wine press* from the fourteenth chapter of Revelation. In later editing, she changed that to *vintage*. But she kept the reference to the wrath of God in 14:19.

She also picks up on themes from Revelation in her reference to trumpets from chapter 7 and to Christ's "terrible swift sword" that was introduced in chapter 1 and will be put to use in chapter 19.

Though slavery is not mentioned by name, it is a subtext in the following lines, originally urging Union soldiers to "die to make men free."[31]

As he died to make men holy
Let us die to make men free
While God is marching on.

As a New York native and long-time resident in New England, she saw slavery as a Christian issue, and she and her husband edited the abolitionist paper, *The Commonwealth*. She was also an advocate for greater freedom for women, including the right to vote.[32] So, perhaps, we can see a logical connection between these freedom issues in the United States Civil War and the church's struggle for freedom throughout Revelation. As the early Christians sought to exercise religious freedom, they risked loss of whatever political freedom they might have had under Rome.

These chapters set the stage for the coming warfare at Armageddon where Christ will do battle against the dragon, the beast, and the false prophet.

Chapter 14

Chapter 13 ended as the beast from the sea put severe restrictions on buying and selling on those who did not have his mark on their hands or their foreheads. Now, without transition or fanfare, 14:1 shifts to the Lamb (who we now recognize is Christ) on Mount Zion (aka Jerusalem) *and with him a hundred and forty-four thousand who had his name and his Father's name written on their foreheads.* So both sides in the cosmic struggle have marks identifying their loyalty. Again, in contrast with the mark of the beast, the followers of the Lamb have His name and His Father's name on their foreheads.

In verses 2-3, we note fluidity of location. Once again, we are in the throne room of heaven where John's vision began in chapters 4-5:

From heaven a mighty voice sounds, variously, *like the sound of many waters and like the sound of loud thunder*; and *like the sound of harpers playing on their harps.* The singers are *the hundred and forty-four thousand who had been redeemed from the earth.* Their new song is one only they can sing. They sing *before the throne and before the four living creatures and before the elders*, whom we met in chapters 4-5.

This heavenly army has a fivefold description:

• *It is these who have not defiled themselves with women, for they are chaste.*

This has been interpreted in at least two ways: (1) In a literal sense, Jewish men going into battle were to abstain from sexual relations with their wives (2 Samuel 11:11, by inference). (2) Spiritually speaking, unfaithfulness to God is often equated with adultery in Scripture. For example, this is the central issue in the book of Hosea. The latter meaning is supported in verse 8 below as Babylon (aka Rome) is said to have *made all nations drink the wine of her impure passion.*

- They *follow the Lamb wherever he goes* (faithful to Christ rather than to the emperor).
- They *have been redeemed from mankind as first fruits for God and the Lamb.* The firstborn animal or human belonged to the Lord (Exodus 13:2). The first fruit or first yield of the harvest belonged to God (Leviticus 2:9-14; Nehemiah 10:35-37). So the hundred forty-four thousand are special to God.
- *No lies were found in their mouths,* in contrast with the lies in the mouth of the beast.
- *For they are spotless.* In the Jewish sacrificial system, lambs for the offering were to be without defect or blemish (Exodus 12:5).

Overall, then, we see followers of the Lamb whom He has saved and purified for a special purpose.

Two Series Of Three Angels

The remainder of chapter 14 is dedicated to two series of three angels. The first trio (verses 6-13) make proclamations. The second three (verses 14-20) call down the harvest of God's wrath into the great wine press.

First Three Angels

First, an angel proclaims to everyone on earth *an eternal gospel*, calling them to *fear God and give him glory for the hour of his judgment has come; and worship him who made heaven and earth, the sea and the fountains of water.*

The second angel proclaims the fall of Babylon as an accomplished fact.

Finally, the third angel declares God's wrath on all those who worshiped the beast and his image and received the mark (that is, those who burned incense at Caesar's altar). They will drink the undiluted wrath of God and be tormented for ever and ever with fire and sulphur in the presence of angels and the Lamb, and they will have no rest, day or night.

With these warnings of judgment on Babylon and worshipers of the beast and his image, we hear *a call for endurance of the saints*. John is told to write, *"Blessed are the dead who die in the Lord henceforth." "Blessed indeed," says the Spirit, "that they may rest from their labors, for their deeds follow them!"*

This is an alert: If they remain faithful and do not receive the mark of the beast (Caesar), they may expect, at the hand of Caesar's agents, to *die in the Lord*.

Second Three Angels

One like a son of man (Christ, see 1:13), seated on a cloud of glory, wears a golden crown of authority and holds a sharp sickle in his hand.

The first angel in this series calls on this One to put in His sickle and begin to reap because the harvest is ripe. So the One seated on the cloud reaps the harvest.

The second angel comes out of the temple in heaven. He, too, has a sharp sickle.

The third and final angel tells the second angel to swing his sickle. This angel gathers the grapes and throws them *into the great wine press of the wrath of God; and the wine press was trodden outside the city, and blood flowed from the wine press, as high as a horse's bridle, for one thousand six hundred stadia.*

In the gory metaphor, God's wrath is the wine press, and the grapes thrown into the press come out as blood rather than grape juice. The blood flows like a river for *one thousand six hundred stadia*, in modern terms, nearly two hundred miles. The river is *as high as a horse's bridle.*

Author John does not mention people being crushed in the wine press, but he borrows from Isaiah 63:1-6, a terrifying picture of angry Yahweh treading on sinful people. Their lifeblood flows out on the earth.

Both John and the ancient prophet speak symbolically of the severity of God's displeasure with those who turn away from Him. In Revelation 14, this is foretaste of horrors to come in chapter 16 when the final round of seven angels rain God's wrath down onto the earth.

Chapter 15: Seven Bowls, But Not Yet

Another portent (a great sign, this one called *great and wonderful*) appears: The seven angels, each with a plague, line up, ready to let them loose upon the earth, and this will be the last because, with them, God's wrath is ended (15:1). But they, and we, have to wait.

Earlier in Revelation, we have seen several dramatic pauses before a climactic event: between the sixth and seventh seals (all of chapter 7), after the seventh seal is opened (8:1), and between the blasts of the sixth and seventh trumpets (10:1-11:14). Chapter 15 provides another pause for dramatic effect before the bowls of wrath are poured out.

We hear music. As with earlier songs, this is a hymn of praise. Though designated as *the song of Moses, the servant of God, and the song of the Lamb*, there are not two clearly delineated songs. In the five books generally attributed to Moses (the Jewish Torah: Genesis through Deuteronomy), two songs are associated with Moses: In Exodus 15, to celebrate the crossing of the Red Sea and the drowning of the Egyptians, Moses sings a long song. In Deuteronomy 32, near the end of his life, Moses sings a song of praise to Yahweh but also tones of vengeance.

The song in Revelation 15 is all together acknowledgement of God's greatness, justice, and holiness (verses 3-4):

"Great and wonderful are thy deeds,
O Lord God the Almighty!
Just and true are thy ways,
O King of the ages!

Who shall not fear and glorify thy name, O Lord?
For thou alone art holy.
All nations shall come and worship thee,
for thy judgments have been revealed."

The singers are those *who had conquered the beast and its image and the number of its name*. The showdown battle is still to come, but here is another indication that, from God's standpoint, the victory over the beast and 666 has already been won.

After this hymn of praise, *the temple of the tent of witness in heaven was opened*. This tent refers to a forerunner of the permanent Temple in Jerusalem, the place of worship as the Israelites wandered in the wilderness, where the presence of Yahweh was felt to dwell in a special way.

Now the seven angels emerge from the temple, and one of the four living creatures gives each angel a golden bowl *full of the wrath of God who lives for ever and ever; and the temple was filled with smoke from the glory of God and from his power, and no one could enter the temple until the seven plagues of the seven angels were ended*. The smoke from the glory of God reflects that awareness of God's special presence in the Tabernacle or tent of witness.

Chapter 16: The Seven Bowls Of Wrath

A loud voice from the temple tells the seven angels to pour out *the seven bowls of the wrath of God*.

The wrath from the first three bowls is quite similar to the havoc brought on as the trumpets sound in chapter 8, but there is greater intensity with the bowls of wrath:

Like the first trumpet, the first bowl brings wrath upon the earth. The first trumpet brought hail, fire, and blood. The first bowl brings sores upon those with the mark of the beast and worshiped his image (burned incense to Caesar).

The second bowl and the second trumpet bring chaos to the sea. The trumpet affects a third of the sea and everything in it, while the second trumpet kills everything in the sea as the sea becomes like the blood of a dead man.

Both the third trumpet and the third bowl contaminate fresh water, but the bowls wreak greater havoc: The third trumpet makes a third of the water bitter. The third bowl turns all the fresh water to blood. The angel of the water then declares God is just in His judgments: Men have shed the blood of saints and prophets; now they are drinking blood. Heaven is silent as to the justice in this comparison.

The fourth angel pours the contents of his bowl on the sun, scorching men with fire and heat. Men curse God for their misery but do not repent.

Bowl five resembles trumpet four as both bring darkness on the earth. Once again, the trumpet scourge is less intense, with one-third of the sun, moon, and stars thrown into darkness. By contrast, bowl number five puts the kingdom of the beast in darkness.

We see more elaborate results with the sixth bowl: The great Euphrates River dries up *to prepare the way for the kings from the east.* Scholars are divided regarding the identity of these Oriental rulers. Perhaps it makes the most sense to link these kings with *the kings of the whole world* noted in verses 13-14:

And I saw, issuing from the mouth of the dragon and from the mouth of the beast and from the mouth of the false prophet, three foul spirits like frogs; for they are demonic spirits, performing signs, who go abroad to the kings of the whole world, to assemble them for battle on the great day of God the Almighty.

The dragon and beast we know from chapters 12-13, each with seven heads and multiple horns and crowns. The false prophet apparently is the lesser beast in the guise of lamb with two horns, the spokesman for the great beast. We see no further mention of this beast, but we will meet this evil trio again at the great battle. The spirits from their mouths are like frogs, a common symbol of evil. These frog-like spirits go out to rally the kings of the whole world for battle against God the Almighty.

Author John issues another alert from Christ to the faithful in verse 15: The Lord is coming unexpectedly, like a thief. They must be alert to His coming and not be caught naked and unprepared. The New Testament has multiple references to Christ's coming as a thief in the night. Here, the reference is simply to a thief. The folks who like to set dates link this to their Rapture.

Then, in verse 16, we have the only time the word *Armageddon* is in Revelation. The wicked trio rally their troops at Armageddon. As on several earlier occasions when the seventh seal and the seventh trumpet are delayed, we might hope now to plunge into the battle. But once again, Author John makes us wait.

Instead of commencing with Armageddon's warfare, the seventh and final bowl of God's wrath pours its contents into the air, and a loud voice comes out of the temple, from the throne, with the message, "It is done." This is accompanied by all manner of natural disaster against Babylon (aka Rome): *And there were flashes of lightning, voices, peals of thunder, and a great earthquake such as had never been since men were on the earth, so great was that earthquake* (verse 18).

Perhaps the "It is done" echoes the words from Jesus on the cross, "It is finished" (John 19:30).

We get a preview of the destruction that falls on Babylon in chapters 17-18. The great city is divided into three parts, (*three* reflecting the divine number), an indication that God's wrath has fallen on the city. Other cities also fall. Babylon is forced to drain the cup of God's fury.

Then John describes additional disaster: As if the physical world flees from the wrath against Babylon, *every island fled away, and no mountains were to be found*. The final blow comes with great hailstones, *heavy as a hundred-weight* dropping on men. This weight has been estimated as ranging from sixty-six pounds to two hundred pounds. Again, we need not take this literally. Rather than puzzle over the size of the hailstones, we should stand amazed at the power of God as suggested in the hail. The sad element here is that men refuse to repent, even amid this destruction.

Rejoice, The Lord Is King

Throughout Revelation, we have seen various songs praising the might and power of the one seated upon the throne and the Lamb who was slain. The prolific eighteenth century composer Charles Wesley, who with his brother John was a founder of Methodism, is credited with writing several thousand hymns. "Rejoice, the Lord is King" is one of many of his hymns reflecting this authority of Christ:

> *Rejoice, the Lord is King!*
> *Your Lord and King adore;*
> *Rejoice, give thanks, and sing,*
> *And triumph evermore;*
> *Lift up your heart, lift up your voice;*
> *Rejoice, again I say, rejoice!*
>
> *Jesus, the Savior, reigns,*
> *The God of truth and love;*
> *When He had purged our stains,*
> *He took His seat above;*
> *Lift up your heart, lift up your voice;*
> *Rejoice, again I say, rejoice!*
>
> *His kingdom cannot fail,*
> *He rules o'er earth and Heav'n,*
> *The keys of death and hell*
> *Are to our Jesus giv'n;*
> *Lift up your heart, lift up your voice;*
> *Rejoice, again I say, rejoice!*
>
> *Rejoice in glorious hope!*
> *Jesus the Judge shall come,*
> *And take His servants up*
> *To their eternal home;*
> *We soon shall hear th' archangel's voice;*
> *The trump of God shall sound, rejoice!*[33]

7 – Revelation, Chapters 17-18: The Fall of Babylon

My name is Ozymandias, king of kings:
Look on my works, ye Mighty, and despair![34]

Percy Bysshe Shelley's lines in his sonnet, "Ozymandias," describe the crumbling remains of a massive monument. These words engraved on the base once struck fear in the hearts of passersby when the statue towered over a town square.

Now, though, the town is gone, and all that remains on the pedestal are "two vast and trunkless legs of stone" sticking up in the air out in a desert. The torso is missing, but a frowning, sneering face, half-covered in the sand, peers up at strangers who pause from their travel.

Later curiosity seekers note irony in the inscription. The self-proclaimed "king of kings" no longer causes "despair" in the hearts of those who read the message from Ozymandias.

Shelley concludes by describing the desolation around the monument built by a powerful, ego-driven man to his own glory. The whole affair is now a "colossal wreck," decaying in "the lone and level sands" that stretch into the distance.[35]

This poem can set the stage for chapters 17-18 of Revelation as they depict the fall of "Babylon." We've noted in earlier chapters, the message of hope permeates Revelation, assuring us the victory already belongs to Christ even though the decisive battle is yet to be fought. For example, in 11:15, *Then the seventh angel blew his trumpet, and there were loud voices in heaven, saying, "The kingdom of the world has become the kingdom of our Lord and of his Christ, and he shall reign for ever and ever."*

Predating Ozymandias, more than one Caesar declared himself

"king of kings," giving reason for the mighty to look on his works and despair. But we soon will see the Lamb (aka Christ) declared Lord of lords and King of kings (17:14 and 19:16). From God's point of view, Christ's foes who threaten Christians already are crumbled, the pagan rulers lying half-buried in the sands of time.

Preview

Through a maze of mixed metaphors, chapter 17 anticipates the fall of Babylon, which we have established is a code name for Rome. Then chapter 18 opens with a mighty voice declaring, "Fallen, fallen is Babylon the great!" But we have no actual account of the fall. Instead, anticipation of the fall continues through much of chapter 18, interspersed with mourning by traders on land and sea who have an unholy alliance with Babylon for their income. In both chapters, Author John depicts this relationship in sexual terms: Babylon apparently is the great harlot who commits fornication with other nations, although Babylon is not named until 18:2-3 in which the same sexual symbolism is used.

The harlot is, variously, *seated upon many waters* (17:1); *sitting on a scarlet beast which was full of blasphemous names, and it had seven heads and ten horns* (17:3); the seven heads are seven mountains on which the woman is seated; they are also seven kings (17:9-10).

The Harlot And The Kings

One of the seven angels who had the seven bowls invites Author John to see *the judgment of the great harlot who is seated upon many waters* (verse 1). Verse 15 explains the waters *are peoples and multitudes and nations and tongues* who depend on Babylon as trading partners. Many of these nations came to Rome by sea.

The central figure of Babylon-Rome as a harlot, in part, reflects widespread worship of Roma, the city's namesake. Also, the Romans worshiped many other gods, including the emperor who made life miserable for faithful Christians. In Jewish and Christian

Scripture, such worship often is labeled as adultery or fornication. It is the harlot *with whom the kings of the earth have committed fornication* and the people of the earth are drunk with the wine of this fornication (verse 2). In modern allusion, people "prostitute themselves" or sell themselves out in the interest of money or fame or other pursuits that occupy them unduly.

John is carried away in the Spirit into a wilderness or desert where he sees *a woman sitting on a scarlet beast which was full of blasphemous names, and it had seven heads and ten horns.* (verse 3). The seven heads and ten horns could identify either the red dragon in chapter 12 or his deputy, the great beast in chapter 13. But the *blasphemous names* point more logically to the beast who represents emperors who call themselves gods. The scarlet remind us of the blood of the faithful who refused to worship the emperor.

We have noted previously, the seven heads of the beast are a series of emperors, and crowns are a symbol of power and authority. Though some interpreters try to identify seven specific emperors, the symbolism of *seven* as completeness may indicate a complete number of wicked rulers who rain terror on Christians.

The woman's purple and scarlet garments indicate royalty, and she wears costly gems: gold and jewels and pearls. She holds a golden cup, consistent with her profligate lifestyle. If we are tempted to take any of this literally, we move to clearly figurative language when we examine her drink: It is not an earthly vintner's product. Rather, the cup is *full of abominations and the impurities* [or filthiness] *of her fornication* (verse 4). She is, in fact, *drunk with the blood of the saints and the blood of the martyrs of Jesus* (verse 6). On her forehead, she is clearly identified for the first time: *Babylon the great, mother of harlots and of earth's abominations* (abominations pertain to idolatry).

The angel further identifies the beast as the one who *was and is not and is to come.* This is another reference to the legend that Nero had come back to life in the form of the current emperor Domitian.

As John does from time to time, he tells his readers that what he is saying *calls for a mind with wisdom* (verse 9). Then he points to Rome, the city set on seven hills, as he says the seven heads of the beast *are seven mountains on which the woman is seated.* This is another obvious symbolic description. If this were literal, we would have a very large woman or very small mountains.

John changes his metaphor again, explaining the seven mountains also are seven kings (verse 10). He goes on in figurative language to cite an eighth king who belongs to the seven, who is headed for perdition or utter destruction (verse 11). Then, he explains, the ten horns *are ten kings who have not yet received royal power.* As before, we need not try to identify these kings other than the popular tradition of Nero's coming back to life.

These last-named ten kings *are to receive authority as kings for one hour, together with the beast.* The span of one hour is used several times in these chapters, each indicating a brief time, but not a literal sixty minutes (verse 12).

All these kings agree to give *their power and authority to the beast.* They will join the beast in making *war on the Lamb* (verses 13-14).

Once more, we are assured of the result of the battle before it begins: *the Lamb will conquer them, for he is Lord of lords and King of kings, and those with him are called and chosen and faithful* (verse 14).

Then we are told, the ten horns (ten kings) and the beast will turn against the harlot: *they will* make her desolate and naked, and devour her flesh and burn her up with fire (verse 16).

As part of God's working all things together for good, Author John says the union of the ten kings with the beast as something God *put into their hearts to carry out his purpose.*

Finally, in the last verse of chapter 17, John identifies the woman as *the great city which has dominion over the kings of the earth* (verse 18).

[*This is a good place to remind ourselves, the Bible was not written in chapters and verses, as explained in the Introduction. Thus, the narrative continues without a break in chapter 18.]*

"Fallen Is Babylon"

Earlier, in 14:8, an angel declared Babylon was fallen – another example of announcement of a coming event as if it had already transpired. Again, in 18:2, another angel, one with great authority and brightness announces, with a mighty voice, *"Fallen, fallen is Babylon the great!"* If Babylon is Rome, this, too, is a prediction. But John is sure the wicked city cannot endure for long.

The angel says the once-great city has become fit only as the habitation for demons, foul spirits, and hateful birds (verse 2) because of the boiling passion and fornication committed by the kings with Babylon. Merchants of the earth also *have grown rich with the wealth of her wantonness* or evil desire (verse 3).

Another voice from heaven calls God's people to leave the center of iniquity, lest they take part in its sins and then suffer the plagues that come as the consequences of sin (verse 4). In heavenly hyperbole, Babylon's sins are so great in number, *they are heaped high as heaven.* Men and women may try to forget their sins, but *God has remembered her iniquities.*

The witness of prophets and apostles is that God Almighty does not forget the sins of those who persist in them:

All we like sheep have gone astray; we have turned every one to his own way (Isaiah 53:6), and *the wages of sin is death* (Romans 6:23). *He who believes in him is not condemned; he who does not believe is condemned already, because he has not believed in the name of the only Son of God. And this is the judgment, that the light has come into the world, and men loved darkness rather than light, because their deeds were evil* (John 3:18-19).

But those same prophets and apostles in the same passages offer hope for the repentant: Isaiah points to the Suffering Servant and declares, *The Lord has laid on him the iniquity of us all* (Isaiah 53:6). The positive side of the death sentence in Romans 6:23 is that *the free gift of God is eternal life through Jesus Christ our Lord.* And John says, *For God so loved the world that he gave his only Son, that whoever believes in him should not perish but have eternal life. For God sent the Son into the world, not to condemn the world, but that the world might be saved through him* (John 3:16-17).

Babylon-Rome is not repentant, so she will be repaid double for her deeds. She has drunk the blood of the martyrs from her golden cup (see 17:6), glorifying herself and playing the wanton, boasting all the while that she sits as a queen, is no widow, and will never see mourning (verses 6-7).

When judgment comes, it will be sudden: *so shall her plagues come in a single day* (18:8). Then, three times over, we are told, judgment will come in one hour (verses 10, 17, and 19). The sins of the great city have accumulated for so long that they are heaped to heaven, apparently without reckoning. But one day, one hour, she will reap her wages. A Baptist minister named R. G. Lee wrote a sermon he called "Pay Day Someday," based on judgment that came to King Ahab and his wicked wife Jezebel – on God's schedule – in First Kings 21-22. Lee is reported to have preached it more than twelve hundred times.[36] The sermon became a showpiece, but the title and central theme of payment for sin are worthy of consideration in the story of Babylon-Rome. The voice from heaven declares, *for mighty is the Lord God who judges her* (verse 8).

Mourning For Babylon

Great weeping and wailing breaks out among kings, merchants, and traders at sea who have benefited from reciprocal arrangements with Babylon when they survey their losses (verses 9-19). We can sense something of the scope of Roman commerce as the merchants weep over wares they can no longer deliver to her shores. Can we detect seven similar groupings of cargo they cry over in verses 12-13?

[1] *gold, silver, jewels and pearls*
[2] *fine linen, purple, silk and scarlet*

[3] *all kinds of scented wood, all articles of ivory, all articles of costly wood, bronze, iron and marble*
[4] *cinnamon, spice, incense, myrrh, frankincense*
[5] *wine, oil, fine flour and wheat*
[6] *cattle and sheep, horses and chariots*
[7] *slaves, that is, human souls*

They mourn not so much for Babylon-Rome as for their loss of income:

And the merchants of the earth weep and mourn for her, since no one buys their cargo any more (verse 11).

And all shipmasters and seafaring men, sailors and all whose trade is on the sea, stood far off and cried out as they saw the smoke of her burning, "What city was like the great city?" And they threw dust on their heads, as they wept and mourned, crying out, "Alas, alas, for the great city where all who had ships at sea grew rich by her wealth!" (verses 17-19).

Call To Rejoice

Those who have suffered at Babylon-Rome's hand are told to rejoice over the great city's fall: *Rejoice over her, O heaven, O saints and apostles and prophets, for God has given judgment for you against her!* (verse 20)

The call for Christians to rejoice should not be over Babylon-Rome's suffering, but rather over the end of their own suffering, in order that righteousness and justice will prevail. Biblical teachings caution against gloating over the suffering of others:

Do not rejoice when your enemy falls, and let not your heart be glad when he stumbles (Proverbs 24:17).

Never avenge yourselves, but leave it to the wrath of God; for it is written, "Vengeance is mine, I will repay, says the Lord" (Romans 12:19).

Do not return evil for evil or reviling for reviling (1 Peter 3:9).

A rabbinic story tells how the Lord delegated some angels to work out a plan for the Israelites to escape from Egypt. After the Israelites were safely across the Red Sea, the Lord heard the angels singing and dancing. When He inquired about the cause for rejoicing, the angels told how they caused the Egyptian army to drown in the sea after Israel crossed on dry land. Then the angels heard God crying. They asked the cause for His tears. He said, "I'm weeping over the death of my children."

An Object Lesson

Writing coaches often emphasize the value of using action verbs to show what a person is doing instead of simply using abstract statements. "Jack was very mad at Sam" is not as effective as "Jack's face flushed deep red as he shook his fist and swore at Sam." This principle is summed up in the slogan: "Show, don't tell."

Hebrew prophets often used object lessons, vividly demonstrating the central point of their messages:

• To show Yahweh's willingness to redeem Israel from its sin, Hosea bought back his wife who had been sold into sexual slavery (Hosea 3:1-5).

• To stress how Egypt would be led away into captivity without clothes, Isaiah walked around naked and barefooted (Isaiah 20:2-6).

• To show how His body would soon be broken and His blood shed, Jesus used bread and wine as vivid demonstration to the disciples (Matthew 26:26-28).

Here in Revelation 18:21, a mighty angel follows the prophets in demonstrating Babylon's being overthrown: *Then a mighty angel took up a stone like a great millstone and threw it into the sea, saying, "So shall Babylon the great city be thrown down with violence, and shall be found no more."*

Signs Of Desolation

The angel who threw the millstone into the sea borrows from Jeremiah 25:10 as he cites five common aspects of daily life in Babylon-Rome that will disappear in the destruction (verses 22-23):

Music: *the sound of harpers and minstrels, of flute players and trumpeters, shall be heard in thee no more;*
Artisans: *a craftsman of any craft shall be found in thee no more;*
Wheat and grain grinding: *the sound of the millstone shall be heard in thee no more;*
Lights at night: *the light of a lamp shall shine in thee no more;*
Weddings: *the voice of bridegroom and bride shall be heard in thee no more;*

This desolation comes as judgment against Babylon-Rome for deceiving the merchants and nations with the black art of sorcery and for shedding the blood of prophets and saints.

Think again of Shelley's obituary for Ozymandias: The once-fear-inspiring statue lay half-covered in the desert dust.

God Moves in a Mysterious Way

Recognizing that Christians often lived in fear under the Roman Empire, Author John, throughout Revelation, pointed them to the power and authority of God through Christ. Frequently things happened beyond their understanding. St. Paul reflected on this when he wrote, *O the depth of the riches and wisdom and knowledge of God! How unsearchable are his judgments and how inscrutable his ways!* (Romans 11:33). William Cowper, a British dramatist and poet, spoke to this mystery in his 1774 poem that found its way into Christian hymnals.

> *God moves in a mysterious way*
> *His wonders to perform;*
> *He plants His footsteps in the sea*
> *And rides upon the storm. . . .*
>
> *Ye fearful saints, fresh courage take;*
> *The clouds ye so much dread*
> *Are big with mercy and shall break*
> *In blessings on your head.*

Judge not the Lord by feeble sense,
But trust Him for His grace;
Behind a frowning providence
He hides a smiling face.

His purposes will ripen fast,
Unfolding every hour;
The bud may have a bitter taste,
But sweet will be the flow'r.

Blind unbelief is sure to err
And scan His work in vain;
God is His own interpreter,
And He will make it plain.[37]

8 – Revelation, Chapter 19: The Battle of Armageddon

The battle at Armageddon is one of the three super-charged topics in Revelation, along with the mark of the beast in chapter 13 and the Millennium in chapter 20. So, to bring Armageddon into proper biblical focus, let's review a basic goal of this book along with guiding principles or "keys" to understanding the biblical text.

An underlying goal of the present writing is to determine what actually is in Revelation and what is not. That is highly desirable as we deal with chapter 19.

Reviewing The Keys

In the Introduction to this present book, I offered "Seven Keys to Unlock the Mysteries of Revelation." Let's summarize those keys.

1. The Historical Setting

Revelation was written late in the First Christian Century when Christians who refused to burn incense at altars to the emperor could face punishment, exile, or death.

2. The Very First Sentence

In this first sentence, John says he has a revelation of "what must soon take place": *The revelation of Jesus Christ, which God gave him to show to his servants what must soon take place . . .*

3. A Message of Hope in Times of Persecution

Letters to seven churches precede the main vision of the book. John writes distinctive messages to each church, comfort or correction as needed. Some of the churches are in the throes of great suffering.

4. Christ the Central Figure

From the early chapters, Jesus Christ is the One with power to conquer evil, from the time He stands among the struggling churches in chapter 1 till He ultimately triumphs over the Devil and his henchmen in chapters 19 and 20.

5. Similarity to Other New Testament Books

It is crucial to realize Revelation is like all other New Testament books in one way: It was written primarily for people who lived in the First Christian Century.

6. Crucial Difference from Other New Testament Books

On the other hand, Revelation stands in sharp contrast with all other New Testament books with its weird creatures, symbolism, and mysterious numbers in a setting of struggle and calamity. Revelation and similar writings are a genre known as *apocalyptic* literature. In fact, the name of this book in the Greek language of the New Testament is *Apocalupsis*, which simply means *revelation*.

7. Obvious Symbolism

Open almost any page in Revelation, and you will find descriptions it is almost impossible to take at face value.

'I Wrote It In'

Once more, I refer you to a dear lady named Amy, now long-deceased, who was so sure Susanna Wesley's statement, "Cleanliness is next to godliness," is in the Bible that she wrote it in her Bible. To her, if it wasn't in the Bible, it should be. Sad to say, many of Amy's friends congregate at chapter 19.

The word *Armageddon* is in the Bible, but not in chapter 19. Back in chapter 16, we saw the dragon, the beast, and the false prophet rallying the kings of the whole world and gathering them at Armageddon, ready to do battle against God. There we left them while we saw the fall of the great evil city, Babylon-Rome, in chapters 17-18.

Now, in chapter 19, we will approach that location whose very name causes many hearts to beat faster and eyes dilate in anticipation of the great war they have been taught will unfold. The battle occupies the final three verses of this chapter.

Before The War

In the first ten verses of chapter 19, we again are in the throne room of heaven where the first sound we hear seems to be *the loud voice of a great multitude in heaven.*

Although singing is not mentioned, we imagine the words they cry out are a magnificent anthem. The first word of their "song" is *Hallelujah*, which in Hebrew means *praise to Yahweh*. Their praise is fourfold, as three additional *hallelujahs* follow.

The great multitude then describe God: *Salvation and glory and power belong to our God, for his judgments are true and just* (verses 1-2). Evidence of God's nature is seen in His judgment of *the great harlot who corrupted the earth with her fornication, and he has avenged on her the blood of his servants.*

Once more the multitude cries, "*Hallelujah! The smoke from her goes up for ever and ever.*"

The third *Hallelujah* comes from those we met in chapter 4 in the throne room: *And the twenty-four elders and the four living creatures fell down and worshiped God who is seated on the throne, saying, "Amen. Hallelujah!"* (verse 4)

Next, an unidentified voice from the throne cries out, "*Praise our God, all you his servants, you who fear him, small and great.*" (verse 5).

The fourth *Hallelujah* (verse 6) is greater in volume and in content: It is like a great multitude, like the sound of many waters and like the sound of mighty thunder peals. Their words have been immortalized musically in George Frederick Handel's oratorio, *Messiah*, using the old familiar King James English: "*Hallelujah! For the Lord God Omnipotent reigneth.*"

After the fourfold *Hallelujah*, the focus shifts (verses 7-9) to preparation for the marriage of the Lamb and His Bride. She has made herself ready. She was granted the privilege of being *clothed with fine linen, bright and pure.* But fine linen is actually *the righteous deeds of the saints.* So this indicates we are not talking about a literal, physical single young lady heading for the wedding altar. Such a young woman would be wearing something more than righteous deeds. As Author John ponders what all this might mean, the angel tells him, *"Write this: Blessed are those who are invited to the marriage supper of the Lamb."* Then the heavenly messenger tells John, *"These are true words of God."*

Most people like weddings. Maybe we are like Mrs. Soames who watches the wedding in Thornton Wilder's *Our Town.* She confesses, "Don't know when I've seen such a lovely wedding. But I always cry. Don't know why it is, but I always cry."[38] Because John is so overwhelmed by all the angel has told him, he falls down to worship the angel. But the angel forbids this: *"You must not do that! I am a fellow servant with you and your brethren who hold the testimony of Jesus. Worship God."*

The Bride in this scene is commonly called "the Bride of Christ," although that precise term is not in the Bible. Even so, the Gospels frequently refer to Christ in parables as the Bridegroom (for example, Matthew 9:15), and Ephesians compares the husband-wife relation to that between Christ and the Church (5:21-32). In the Hebrew Scriptures, Isaiah uses the bridegroom figure for God (62:5). In all these instances, the intimacy between husband and wife as a picture of the Christian's closeness to Christ has inspired the faithful across the centuries. So the general assumption is that the Bride is the Church.

Christ The Conqueror

Immediately on the heels of the bridegroom language, Christ appears – not as a bridegroom, but riding a white horse as the leader of the armies of heaven, (verse 11).

We saw another warrior on a white horse in chapter 6, as the first seal on the scroll was opened, but that warrior brought only death. Christ is called Faithful and True, and He goes in righteousness as He judges and makes war (verse 11). Shortly, we will see the nature of His war.

The additional descriptions of Christ (verses 12-16) pick up on various references in earlier chapters:
- *His eyes are like a flame of fire* (1:14).
- On his head are many diadems. No number of crowns is given, but *many* is more than the *seven* on the red dragon (12:3) or the *ten* on the great beast (13:1).
- He will rule the nations with a rod of iron (2:27; 12:5).
- He will tread the wine press of the fury of the wrath of God the Almighty (14:18-20).
- He wears the name *King of kings and Lord of lords* (17:14).
- *From his mouth issues a sharp sword with which to smite the nation*s.

This sword first appeared in 1:16, and we recall, if a playwright or novelist introduces a gun or sword at an early point in the plot, this is a *foreshadowing*. The audience or reader will make a mental note to expect to see the weapon put to use before the story ends. As we will see almost momentarily, that sword in chapter 1 was a foreshadowing of things to come at Armageddon.

The Armies Of Heaven

Before going further, we need to pause to notice the armies of heaven who ride with Christ as they are described in verse 14:

And the armies of heaven, arrayed in fine linen, white and pure, followed him on white horses.

The warriors are not in traditional battle garb. They wear no protective armor. They carry no weapons. Of course, these are the *armies of heaven*, not men of the earth. There are no tanks. There are no helicopters. There are no drone missiles. There are no nukes. Again, they carry no weapons.

Invitation To Supper

We pause once more before we arrive at the battle scene. In verses 17-18, we hear a supper invitation for birds of prey to feast on the carnage of the approaching battle:

Then I saw an angel standing in the sun, and with a loud voice he called to all the birds that fly in midheaven, "Come, gather for the great supper of God, to eat the flesh of kings, the flesh of captains, the flesh of mighty men, the flesh of horses and their riders, and the flesh of all men, both free and slave, both small and great."

We will see the outcome of this invitation in verse 21.

Finally, The Battle!

Now, three verses (19-21) tell all we know about the battle at Armageddon.

Recall first the armies we met in 16:14-16.

And I saw the beast and the kings of the earth with their armies gathered to make war against him who sits upon the horse and against his army.

Then two evil figures – the beast and the false prophet – are captured and disposed of:

And the beast was captured, and with it the false prophet who in its presence had worked the signs by which he deceived those who had received the mark of the beast and those who worshiped its image. These two were thrown alive into the lake of fire that burns with sulphur.

That takes care of two battle strategists. Now, in one lone verse, we see what happens to their armies:

And the rest were slain by the sword of him who sits upon the horse, the sword that issues from his mouth; and all the birds were gorged with their flesh.

That sword we have anticipated since chapter 1 swings into action. With it, Christ slays all the other warriors, and the birds who were invited to supper begin to gorge themselves with the flesh of the slain.

But once again, we must look closely at that sword. This sword is not a weapon of steel. It *issues from his mouth.* It is the mighty word of Christ. Remember, the armies of heaven are dressed in fine linen, with no indication of shields, armor, or weapons. So the sword – the mighty word of Christ – is the one weapon that slays all the evil enemies.

This is not flesh and blood fighting. John is saying the word of Christ has overcome all evil.

On that basis, then, we also logically have figurative language rather than a literal bloody feast as the birds gorge themselves on the flesh of the kings and their armies and their horses. If you thought Revelation was building up to a blood-and-guts battle with weapons of mass destruction, this may seem anti-climactic. If you expect fierce battles with guns and tanks and missiles and helicopters and drones, you need to look somewhere other than in Revelation to find it. That kind of warfare is simply not here.

If you read the *Left Behind* books or see their movies, keep this in mind: Everything they say about the Battle of Armageddon is pure fiction. Well, maybe not pure, but all fiction. Their great military buildup simply is not there. The *Left Behind* industry and so much of what you hear from preachers on radio and TV about the end of the world has no biblical basis.

You needn't feel let down or disappointed. You and Amy should put down your ballpoint pens once for all and not write in details Author John leaves out.

We have just reviewed everything the Bible says about the Battle of Armageddon, and we have seen the only weapon is the sword of Christ's word which comes from His mouth. Forget the rest, unless you just want to be entertained by a novel or a movie.

This is the most positive message in heaven or on earth: The word from the mouth of Christ is powerful against all the forces of evil.

Lead On, O King Eternal

In the wake of Armageddon, various hymns of Christian warfare come to mind. Unless we examine them closely, some of these might seem to encourage actual military combat. "Onward, Christian Soldiers" and "The Banner of the Cross" have been criticized — perhaps unduly — in this regard. But the middle stanza of 1888 hymn, "Lead on, O King Eternal" by Ernest W. Shurtleff comes closest to the spirit of Christ at Armageddon as He uses no physical weapons:

Lead on, O King eternal,
Till sin's fierce war shall cease,
And holiness shall whisper
The sweet amen of peace.
For not with swords' loud clashing,
Nor roll of stirring drums;
With deeds of love and mercy
The heavenly kingdom comes.[39]

9 – Revelation, Chapter 20: The Millennium and the Final Judgment

The Millennium

> "My time is your time
> Your time is my time . . .
> There's no time like our time."[40]

Rudy Vallee adopted "My Time is Your Time" by Eric Little as the theme song for his network radio show from the 1920s into the 1940s.[41]

As we continue reading Revelation, keep in mind, our time may not be the same as God's eternal time, and calculations of time in Revelation are highly symbolic.

Those who prefer to take the numbers in Revelation at face value get very excited over the thousand years of peace in chapter 20. This period is known as the *Millennium* because the Latin word for *one thousand* is *millennium.* In this instance, it is a thousand years of peace following the decisive defeat of the forces of the beast and the false prophet and their armies at Armageddon, victory that came through the use of one weapon: the two-edged sword of the word of Christ.

For those who follow the literalism of the Darby-Scofield system, the *Millennium* is the grand thousand-year climax to the sequence that began with the Rapture.

Seizing Satan – Verses 1-3

As a prelude to the thousand years of peace, an angel from heaven comes carrying the key to the bottomless pit, along with a great chain. The angel seizes the chief of evil who – here as when we first met him in chapter 12 – is identified as the dragon, the serpent, the Devil and Satan. In fourfold manner, the angel exercises control over Satan: He binds evil one for a thousand years, throws him into the bottomless pit, shuts the pit, and seals it (verses 1-3) so that Satan can no longer deceive the nations regarding the emperor as a god. For reasons Author John does not explain, Satan will be allowed to run loose again for a time after the thousand years elapse.

In our ongoing comparison of literal versus symbolic, think a moment about binding Satan. Is he a physical or a spiritual being? If he is not physical, what kind of chain will it take to bind him? Wouldn't we more wisely see this as symbolic of God's control over the center of evil?

Also consider *the bottomless pit*. Another translation is a more general description, *the abyss*. If *bottomless* is accurate, how literally would we expect to find a pit with no bottom? How would such a pit be sealed over in such a way that Satan could not escape? The real point is not the nature of the chain or of the pit but the power of God to control and ultimately destroy the power of evil. And the thousand years need not be considered literal any more than the chain.

The Thousand-Year Reign – Verses 4-6

Darby-Scofield calls for Jesus to return physically to Jerusalem for this thousand-year reign and set up a throne to rule with those who were taken up into heaven in the Rapture and escape the Great Tribulation. Verse 4, however, is not entirely clear as to who the people are who reign with Christ in the Millennium. Two groups are indicated, with identity of the second group not left in doubt:

Also I saw the souls of those who had been beheaded for their testimony to Jesus and for the word of God, and who had not worshiped the beast or its image and had not received its mark on their foreheads or their hands. They came to life, and reigned with Christ a thousand years.

These are martyred Christians who stood fast in worshiping the one true God, the Father of the Lord Jesus Christ. They were not raptured up into heaven alive. They were murdered here on earth.

Who are the first group? *Then I saw thrones, and seated on them were those to whom judgment was committed.* Author John does not explain further who these people are. So, perhaps we should not worry about their identities. Our rapturous friends see themselves seated on thrones with Christ for the Millennium, reigning with Him for the thousand years (verse 6).

Defeat Of The Devil – Verses 7-10

When the thousand years are over, Satan is let loose. He gathers his forces from *the four corners of the earth, that is, Gog and Magog, to gather them for battle; their number is like the sand of the sea.*

Earlier in Revelation 7, we noted the flat-earth understanding, with angels standing at the four corners of the earth, holding back ill winds. Here, Satan goes to those same areas to find his supporters (verse 8). John borrows the names of Gog and Magog from Ezekiel 38-39. There, Gog is *the chief prince* (king?) the prophet preaches against. Gog is from the unidentified land of Magog. This reference whets the imaginations of those who expect to see these folks siding with Satan in one more pitched battle before Satan is permanently removed. Their number is almost endless. Perhaps some would identify them with the two hundred million cavalrymen in 9:16. Satan's troops march over the earth and surround the saints and the beloved city, Jerusalem, but fire comes down from heaven and consumes them (20:9). Satan is not flesh and blood, so, as with Christ's destruction of evil at Armageddon, the final round with Satan is spiritual warfare.

As the final blow to the power of evil, the Devil is thrown into the lake of fire where his partners in evil, the beast and the false prophet, have been since their defeat at Armageddon (19:21).

Everything about Satan in this chapter – and in the entire book of Revelation – shows Satan is not all-powerful. Satan is not a bad god on equal footing with the one true God. Satan is a rebel who Author John sees finally, ultimately defeated and cast away forever.

Further Thoughts On The Millennium

For several decades, it was common to discuss three general approaches to the Millennium: Premillennial, Postmillennial, and Amillennial. The prefixes *pre-* and *post-* refer to when Christ is expected to return. As the prefix suggests, Premillennialists say Christ will come *before* the reign of peace. This viewpoint usually embodies the sequence of the Darby-Scofield scheme.

Postmillennialists say Christ will come back *after* a thousand years of peace, but this view has had various shades of meaning. During the nineteenth century, many theologians felt they saw signs of progress in society at large and believed this would continue. They interpreted this progress as a sign the Millennium had arrived and Christ would return at the end of the thousand years. But they were slow to project a date for fulfillment of this expectation. This rosy outlook lost its glow as world events moved toward what was called The Great War, that began in 1914 (World War One), the one that was supposed to end all wars. The Postmillennial name has continued to the present, but for many, if not most, the concept has taken on a definite symbolic interpretation. The idea is that Christian teaching and preaching will eventually usher in a new age of peace but not with the literal embellishments of Premillennialism.

Amillennialism is akin to Postmillennialism in rejecting the Darby-Scofield interpretation. The Greek prefix *a-* means *no* or *not*, so this outlook rejects a literal thousand years of peace, either before or after Christ's return to judge the world and claim His own.

A more recent classification of eschatology offers a simpler approach and simpler terminology with only two categories: literal and symbolic. You can see how the historic systems fall under this twofold classification. By now, it should be obvious, this present book is committed to a symbolic understanding of Revelation and other biblical passages often brought to bear on interpretation of the end time.

More On Literal Versus Symbolic

Often when someone says, "I take the Bible literally," he/she really means, "I take the Bible seriously. I believe it really is true."

Premillennialists often say they take Revelation and other eschatological passages literally, but it is beyond belief that they actually envision the red dragon with a tail that knocks a third of the stars out of the sky (chapter 12) or that the Babylonian harlot sits on seven hills (chapter 17). But they defend to the death the Millennium as a literal thousand years.

This chapter on the Millennium began with Rudy Vallee's theme song, "My time is your time." Accompanying this was the thought that God's time does not necessarily run on our time. Two Bible passages – one from the Old Testament, one from the New Testament, may help us at this point:

Psalm 90:4 – *For a thousand years in thy sight are but as yesterday when it is past, or as a watch in the night.*

2 Peter 3:8-10 – *But do not ignore this one fact, beloved, that with the Lord one day is as a thousand years, and a thousand years as one day. The Lord is not slow about his promise as some count slowness, but is forbearing toward you, not wishing that any should perish, but that all should reach repentance. But the day of the Lord will come like a thief, and then the heavens will pass away with a loud noise, and the elements will be dissolved with fire, and the earth and the works that are upon it will be burned up.*

Can literalist and non-literalists alike agree that, whatever we make of the thousand years in Revelation 20, God's time may not be our time? That, from God's perspective, the anticipated thousand years of peace may pass in a moment with God? That God will bring His peace when He is ready? That He ultimately is in control and does not depend on our interpretation of time? That God does not rely on those Premillennialists who encourage warfare in the Middle East in hope of igniting their imagined Battle of Armageddon with helicopters, tanks, and drones?

Finally, a symbolic reading of the Millennium should take nothing from the urgency of the individual to be ready to meet Christ, whether in the air or in death. Or, in keeping with the central message of Revelation, symbolic reading should take nothing away from the call to members in all the churches to stand with Christ, whether the faithful Christians at Smyrna and Philadelphia or the straying Christians at Sardis or Laodicea.

Jesus Shall Reign Where'er The Sun

Isaac Watts was a prolific hymn writer in England in the eighteenth century. The following hymn envisions a worldwide kingdom under the sway of Christ such as might be envisioned in the Millennium:

Jesus shall reign where'er the sun
Does his successive journeys run,
His kingdom stretch from shore to shore
Till moons shall wax and wane no more.

For Him shall endless prayer be made,
And endless praises crown His head;
His name, like sweet perfume, shall rise
With ev'ry morning sacrifice.

People and realms of ev'ry tongue
Dwell on His love with sweetest song;
And infant voices shall proclaim
Their early blessings on His name.

Blessings abound where'er He reigns;
The pris'ner leaps, unloosed his chains,
The weary find eternal rest,
And all the sons of want are blest.

Where He displays His healing power,
Death and the curse are known no more;
In Him the tribes of Adam boast
More blessings than their father lost.

Let every creature rise and bring
Peculiar honors to our King;
Angels descend with songs again,
And earth repeat the loud Amen.[42]

The Final Judgment

The God that holds you over the pit of hell, much as one holds a spider, or some loathsome insect over the fire, abhors you, and is dreadfully provoked.[43]

Colonial preacher Jonathan Edwards used this analogy in his 1741 sermon, "Sinners in the Hands of an Angry God," warning of judgment to come. I never heard Edwards's name called in the small, mostly rural, churches I attended in childhood and youth. Still, as Daddy moved from farm job to farm job in the area around Sweetwater, Texas, I had a fairly steady diet of sermons on the Last Judgment: Jesus may come at any time. If you died tonight, would you go to heaven or hell?

The New Testament has dozens of references to God's judgment, so it is a well-established Christian teaching. Even so, Revelation's account of the final judgment is told in only five verses. This brevity takes nothing from the significance of the teaching that everyone must stand before God one day to face the deeds he/she has done and to learn his/her eternal destiny. But, as with other flash points we have examined in Revelation, this limited discussion of God's judgment might suggest Amy's Army once again has been at work, developing elaborate scenarios advanced by literalists.

Throughout Revelation, we have seen the book is rich with symbolism, and symbols point to great truths in less-than-literal language. After we examine the verses about judgment (20:11-15), we will look at the symbolic language and the significance of the symbols:

[11] Then I saw a great white throne and him who sat upon it; from his presence earth and sky fled away, and no place was found for them. [12] And I saw the dead, great and small, standing before the throne, and books were opened. Also another book was opened, which is the book of life. And the dead were judged by what was written in the books, by what they had done. [13] And the sea gave up the dead in it, Death and Hades gave up the dead in them, and all were judged by what they had done. [14] Then Death and Hades were thrown into the lake of fire. This is the second death, the lake of fire; [15] and if any one's name was not found written in the book of life, he was thrown into the lake of fire.

Author John sees *a great white throne*, significant of greatness and power (verse 11). Also he sees the being designated only as *him who sat upon it*. This expression calls to mind John's reluctance (in chapters 4-5) to use the name of God.

John personifies earth and heaven: They flee in fear from before the presence of the Almighty (verse 11): *from his presence earth and sky fled away.*

They disappear (verse 11): *and no place was found for them.* This is to make way for the new heaven and new earth which will come in chapter 21.

With the disappearance of the earth and heavens, where is the *great white throne* set up? All the people of the earth, from all time, are gathered in judgment (verses 12-13). So, if the earth literally disappears, where do all these people stand? Author John isn't concerned about such questions because this event isn't about geography. It's about accountability and judgment.

The dead are all there: great and small, those who died at sea, and those in the realm of Death and Hades (the Greek term for the abode of the dead).

Books were opened (verse 12), *And the dead were judged by*

what was written in the books, by what they had done. Also another book was opened, which is the book of life; (verses 12, 15) *and if any one's name was not found written in the book of life, he was thrown into the lake of fire.*

Looking ahead to 21:4, we learn death shall be no more in the new Jerusalem. Death is not part of God's plan. He is the God of life, not of death. So here, in 20:14, Death and Hades are thrown into the lake of fire. Though we just noticed, these two represent the realm of the dead, here they are personified. You may recall, in chapter 6, they were among the four horsemen. Here, as they are thrown into the lake of fire, they join the unholy trinity: the dragon, the beast, and the false prophet (19:10) to remain there forever and ever.

In keeping with the figurative nature of Revelation, we need to ask whether the lake of fire is literal fire as we know it. The general assumption in the New Testament is that we will be changed from physical beings into spiritual. For example, in First Corinthians 15, St. Paul goes to great lengths to emphasize there are all sorts of bodies: humans, animals, birds, fish, sun, moon, and stars (verses 39-41). He says emphatically of the human body: *It is sown a physical body, it is raised a spiritual body* (verse 44). He also says, *we shall all be changed* (verse 51). If this is *literal* fire, it must be a different kind of fire in order to burn spiritual bodies. Is it more likely a burning within our spirits as we look back in remorse over what we have done or left undone?

Many preachers, in the tradition of Jonathan Edwards, seem to enjoy verbally dangling sinners over the fires of hell, rather than sorrowing over those whose names are not written in the book of life. Perhaps trying to "scare the hell out of them" in order to "scare them out of hell." Seminary students, in homiletics classes, prepare and present sermons for their professor and classmates. In one class, as the professor evaluated a sermon on hell, he pointed out the student preacher had smiled a great deal as he preached on the horrors of torment.

Two Hymns

Hymn writer Will L. Thompson struck a sensitive, sensible balance regarding the final judgment: In 1887, he wrote "There's a Great Day Coming," emphasizing the day "When the saints and the sinners shall be parted right and left" and "When the sinner shall hear his doom: 'Depart, I know you not!'" But Thompson did not gloat over the doomed sinner: In 1880, he also wrote "Softly and tenderly Jesus is calling . . . calling, O sinner, come home." Consider the lyrics of the two songs.

There's a Great Day Coming

There's a great day coming, a great day coming;
There's a great day coming by and by,
When the saints and the sinners shall be parted right and left,
Are you ready for that day to come?

There's a bright day coming, a bright day coming;
There's a bright day coming by and by.
But its brightness shall only come to them that love the Lord.
Are you ready for that day to come?

There's a sad day coming, a sad day coming;
There's a sad day coming by and by,
When the sinner shall hear his doom: "Depart, I know you not!"
Are you ready for that day to come?

Are you ready? Are you ready?
Are you ready for the judgment day?
Are you ready? Are you ready
For the judgment day?[44]

Softly and Tenderly
Softly and tenderly Jesus is calling,
Calling for you and for me;
See, on the portals He's waiting and watching,
Watching for you and for me.

Why should we tarry when Jesus is pleading,
Pleading for you and for me?/
Why should we linger and heed not His mercies,
Mercies for you and for me?

Time is now fleeting, the moments are passing,
Passing from you and from me;
Shadows are gathering, deathbeds are coming,
Coming for you and for me.

Oh, for the wonderful love He has promised,
Promised for you and for me!
Though we have sinned, He has mercy and pardon,
Pardon for you and for me.

Come home, come home,
You who are weary, come home;
Earnestly, tenderly, Jesus is calling,
Calling, O sinner, come home![45]

10 – Revelation, Chapters 21-22: The New Jerusalem and Final Words

The New Jerusalem (21:1-22:5)

A thing of beauty is a joy for ever:
Its loveliness increases; it will never
Pass into nothingness...[46]

John Keats was thinking of the beauty of early nineteenth century England when he wrote these lines, but they catch the essence of *the holy city, new Jerusalem*, the climatic vision in this book of visions.

Through most of the verses in the final two chapters of Revelation, we sense everlasting beauty beyond description, as if John of the Apocalypse is an organist pulling out all the stops in the final recital piece for his seven churches. Those churches face persecution and threats of death as they resist pressure to burn incense to the emperor. From time to time in the writing, John has challenged them to live faithfully for Christ. He has shown them how Christ will conquer evil with the power of His word (chapter 19), bringing peace and finally conquering Satan (chapter 20). Now, he points them to the blessed hope of a day when all things will be new. Then, occasionally, John will issue a word of warning, a challenge to be faithful.

The Beauty Of God's Presence

The old earth and sky vanished to make way for God and His great white throne and, ultimately, for the new heaven and new earth (20:11). Now, we will see the beauty of unbroken fellowship with God Himself in the new Jerusalem:

We see the beauty of the holy city *coming down out of heaven from God, prepared as a bride adorned for her husband.* In the eyes of a soon-to-be husband, nothing is so beautiful as his bride on their wedding day.

A voice from the throne proclaims the most beautiful aspect of the new Jerusalem: *and I heard a loud voice from the throne saying, "Behold, the dwelling of God is with men. He will dwell with them, and they shall be his people, and God himself will be with them"* (verse 3).

The Greek word for *dwell* and *dwelling* refers to the Jewish tabernacle, the tent the Israelites took with them during their wilderness wanderings. As the precursor of the sacred Temple, the tabernacle was thought to be the special dwelling place of their God Yahweh (seen frequently in Exodus). In John 1:14, that same word describes Jesus's coming to earth. He dwelt, He pitched His tent, He "tabernacled" among the people He came to save. That meaning carries over in this verse: God is spreading His tent, His tabernacle, over His people, so they may dwell in safety and security under its protection. He is ever-present with them. The people who have been faithful to Christ, who have not worshiped Caesar, shall be God's people *and God himself will be with them.*

In God's dwelling, there will be no more sorrow: *he will wipe away every tear from their eyes, and death shall be no more, neither shall there be mourning nor crying nor pain any more, for the former things have passed away* (verse 4).

As Author John is drawing his book to a close, he picks up on a number of statements from the early chapters, reemphasizing points and completing a circle of thought.

- Verse 5: *And he who sat upon the throne said, "Behold, I make all things new." Also he said, "Write this, for these words are trustworthy and true."*
- In chapters 4-5, God is called, simply, *the one seated on the throne.*
- Christ (in 3:14) calls Himself the *faithful and true* as He writes to the Laodicean church (*Faithful* and *trustworthy* are the same Greek word).

- Those same words describe Christ as He rides to Armageddon (19:11).
- An angel again tells John the words he has received are *trustworthy and true* in 22:6.
- Also in 22:6, the angel repeats words from the very first verse in the book. The message tells *what must soon take place*, rather than thousands of years down the future.
- The voice from the throne says in 21:6, *I am the Alpha and the Omega, the beginning and the end.* Christ calls Himself *the Alpha and the Omega* in 1:8. That identity comes again in 22:13. Alpha and Omega are the first and last letters of the Greek alphabet, so these are yet other declarations of the unceasing presence of God the Father and Christ the Son, the Lamb.

Blessings And Warnings

- In letters to each of the seven churches (chapters 2-3), Christ promises special blessings to those who conquer in His name. God makes a similar promise in 21:7, *He who conquers shall have this heritage, and I will be his God and he shall be my son.*
- Christ found it necessary to warn most of those seven churches: They would be punished if they did not change their unfaithful ways. Here, in 21:8, after the description of God's nearness, John issues the first warning of this closing section:

But as for the cowardly, the faithless, the polluted, as for murderers, fornicators, sorcerers, idolaters, and all liars, their lot shall be in the lake that burns with fire and sulphur, which is the second death.

The cowardly and faithless are those who denied their Lord under persecution. The polluted and fornicators are those who were involved with the harlot (Babylon-Rome), bowing to emperor worship.

Even in the midst of the promise of blessings in the new Jerusalem, John gives additional warnings, because he still is concerned that those early Christians remain faithful: (21:27; 22:11-12; 22:15; and 22:18-19).

A Beautiful City

Many angels have been tour guides for John in his visions. Now, one of the angels who had the bowls of wrath comes to show John *the Bride, the wife of the Lamb* (21:9). Just before Christ (the Lamb) did battle using His sword at Armageddon, we were told of the marriage (19:7-9):

"Let us rejoice and exult and give him the glory, for the marriage of the Lamb has come, and his Bride has made herself ready; it was granted her to be clothed with fine linen, bright and pure" – for the *fine linen is the righteous deeds of the saints. And the angel said to me, "Write this: Blessed are those who are invited to the marriage supper of the Lamb." And he said to me, "These are true words of God."*

In the Spirit, the angel carries John to a high mountain where John sees, not a blushing lady, but *the holy city Jerusalem coming down out of heaven from God.*

John does not explain what the holy city is, other than the dwelling of God and His people. From its description, we think of it as heaven, but John saw it *coming down out of heaven from God*, so it is not identical with heaven.

In the earlier chapter on Armageddon, we noted the Christian Church is traditionally called the Bride of Christ. So we will assume the holy city, Jerusalem, is the Church perfected in heaven, brought down from heaven, and reflecting the fullness of heaven.

- The holy city is beautiful: *having the glory of God, its radiance LIKE a most rare jewel, LIKE a jasper, clear as crystal* (21:11).
- The holy city is perfect: Two numbers of perfection and completeness – twelve and seven – are joined. Twelve is the heavenly number three multiplied by the earthly number four, and there are seven examples of twelves: twelve gates, twelve angels at the gates, and names of the twelve tribes of Israel inscribed on the gates (21:12-13); twelve foundations for the city wall, with names of the twelve apostles of the Lamb on the foundations (21:14); foursquare, twelve thousand stadia in length, breadth, and height – about fifteen hundred miles each way

(21:16); and the wall twelve cubits by twelve cubits – one hundred forty-four – or about two hundred sixteen feet (21:17). There is no indication whether the measure of the wall was its width or its height.
- The holy city is ornate: The city wall is made of the semiprecious jasper stone. The city itself is pure gold (21:18). Each of the twelve foundations is adorned with jewels: *jasper, sapphire, agate, emerald,* onyx, carnelian, chrysolite, beryl, topaz, chrysoprase, jacinth, and amethyst (21:19-20).
- Each of the gates is made of a single pearl. If we have any question about symbolism here, consider the size of the oysters it would take to make those pearls.
- The streets are paved with gold (21:21).
- The holy city needs no temple: On earth, the devout go to buildings dedicated to focusing on God. But *the Lord God the Almighty and the Lamb* are ever with their people, so there is no need to go to a building (21:22; 22:3). Does this not mitigate against the Premillennial expectation of rebuilding an earthly Temple in Jerusalem during the millennial reign?
- The holy city is a place of light: *And the city has no need of sun or moon to shine upon it, for the glory of God is its light, and its lamp is the Lamb* (21:23; 22:5). God and the Lamb illumine the nations, the kings of the world are drawn to the city, and *there shall be no night there.* (21:24-26).

[In the midst of these descriptions, another warning comes as to who will be and who will not be in the holy city: *But nothing unclean shall enter it, nor any one who practices abomination or falsehood, but only those who are written in the Lamb's book of life* (21:27).]
- The holy city has a river: It is *the river of the water of life, bright as crystal,* and it flows *from the throne of God and of the Lamb through the middle of the street of the city.* The hymn, "Shall We Gather at the River," is based on this description. Water is essential to life, but this is the water of eternal life (22:1-2a).
- The holy city gives nourishment and healing: *on either side of*

the river, the tree of life with its twelve kinds of fruit, yielding its fruit each month; and the leaves of the tree were for the healing of the nations* (22:2b). The twelve fruits give spiritual nourishment, and the leaves complete the healing of this world's wounds.
- The holy city's residents see God face to face: *they shall see his face* (22:4). This is significant because Moses asked to see God's face, but God refused to let him (Exodus 33:20). St. Paul uses this figure in First Corinthians 13:12 *For now we see in a mirror dimly, but then face to face. Now I know in part; then I shall understand fully, even as I have been fully understood.*
- The holy city's residents have Christ's identity mark: *his name shall be on their foreheads*. In chapters 13-14, the mark of the beast, 666, is on the foreheads of those who worship the beast-emperor, but the seal of Christ is on the perfect number of disciples, the one hundred, forty-four thousand who have remained faithful. Here in the last chapter of Revelation, Christ's name on foreheads is God's seal of approval.

The Pearly White City

Arthur F. Ingler's song about John's vision of the Holy City, written in 1902, embodies much of the text from Revelation 21:

There's a holy and beautiful city
Whose builder and ruler is God;
John saw it descending from Heaven,
When Patmos, in exile, he trod;
Its high, massive wall is of jasper,
The city itself is pure gold;
And when my frail tent here is folded,
Mine eyes shall its glory behold.

No sin is allowed in that city
And nothing defiling or mean;

No pain and no sickness can enter,
No crepe on the doorknob is seen;
Earth's sorrows and cares are forgotten,
No tempter is there to annoy;
No parting words ever are spoken,
There's nothing to hurt or destroy.

No heartaches are known in that city,
No tears ever moisten the eyes;
There's no disappointment in Heaven,
No envy and strife in the sky;
The saints are all sanctified wholly,
They live in sweet harmony there;
My heart is now set on that city,
And some day its blessings I'll share.

My loved ones are gathering yonder,
My friends too are passing away,
And soon I shall join their bright number,
And dwell in eternity's day;
They're safe now in glory with Jesus,
Their trials and battles are past.
They overcame sin and the tempter,
They've reached that fair city at last.

In that bright city, pearly white city,
I have a mansion, a harp, and a crown;
Now I am watching, waiting, and longing,
For the white city that's soon coming down.[47]

Final Words (22:6-22)

Revelation As Drama

When collegiate or community theater groups complete their final performance of a play, it often falls the lot of the cast and production crew to "strike the set" — taking apart any sets that are not permanently in place on the stage, returning costumes and props to their storage areas, and generally clearing the stage for whatever comes next. But before the audience leaves the theater, there's a curtain call with actors coming out to take their bow.

In *Revelation as Drama*, the late Dr. James L. Blevins, structured his interpretation of Revelation as a theatrical production in seven acts and seven scenes in each act. This forms the outline of his commentary.[48] Then, the book concludes with the script for a drama for churches to present, based on the book.[49] In this passage, Dr. Blevins has speeches by John, an Angel, and an offstage Voice, along with singing by a Choir. The offstage Voice is Jesus.

In a sense, these final seventeen verses of the book of Revelation resemble the end of a live theatrical run. The vision has ended, and Author John is ready to dismantle the whole thing. But we might imagine some of the people associated with the vision coming down to the footlights and speaking to us in the audience, as cast members occasionally do.

If we can imagine that dramatization, we can hear the words of the Angel in verse 6:

These words are trustworthy and true. And the Lord, the God of the spirits of the prophets, has sent his angel to show his servants what must soon take place.

We recognize those last five words are repeated from the very first sentence in Revelation: *what must soon take place.* And we repeat: John is writing about things he fully expects to happen *soon*.

In Dr. Blevins's script, Jesus then speaks from offstage, declaring, "I am coming soon." In the drama, as in Scripture, Jesus says that three times over.[50] Some New Testament scholars say this can also be translated, *I am coming suddenly* or *unexpectedly*. In either translation, this is a call for readiness to listen to the voice of Jesus and be ready for His return. Jesus also declares a blessing on the person who keeps the words of the prophecy of this book.

John identifies himself by name, as he did in the first verse in the book, as the person who heard and saw what he is relaying to those seven churches who are under fire from Caesar. He confesses that he fell down and worshiped the Angel who brought the message from Christ. But, in the same manner as with another angel in 19:10, the heavenly messenger says he is like John, only a fellow servant with John and other prophets and those who keep the words of this book. John is to worship God and not anyone else.

The angel then tells John, *"Do not seal up the words of the prophecy of this book, for the time is near. Let the evildoer still do evil, and the filthy still be filthy, and the righteous still do right, and the holy still be holy"* (22:10-11).

This call to leave the book open is another reminder that John is writing for his own generation. He is not to seal it up to be opened in some later century. John is to deliver the message and let the words fall where they may. He is not responsible for listener response. The evildoer may still do evil, the filthy may remain filthy, the righteous still do righteousness, and the holy still be holy.

Jesus speaks again: *"Behold, I am coming soon, bringing my recompense, to repay every one for what he has done. I am the Alpha and the Omega, the first and the last, the beginning and the end"* (22:12-13). In this threefold message, He says again, He is coming soon or suddenly; He is the judge who will mete out reward or punishment; He is the Alpha and the Omega, the everlasting One, first, last, and always.

In the Blevins script, the Choir sings verses 14-15:

Blessed are those who wash their robes, that they may have the right to the tree of life and that they may enter the city by the gates. Outside are the dogs and sorcerers and fornicators and murderers and idolaters, and every one who loves and practices falsehood.

The presence of the tree of life in the holy city reconnects us with Genesis 2:9; 3:22-24. After Adam and Eve sinned, they were prevented from eating from the tree of life. But in the holy city, the tree of life again is available to everyone in the city. That tree with its twelve fruits is for the healing of the nations, the completion of God's provision for redemption, for God's salvation.

These verses also recall chapter 7 when John saw a multitude beyond number who had washed their robes and made them white in the blood of the Lamb. Those who have washed are now eligible to eat from the tree of life. They may enter the holy city by the gates, rather than having to try to slip in after the manner of those outside the gate: dogs, sorcerers, fornicators, murderers, idolaters, and liars.

Jesus then reasserts Himself as the source of the testimony for the churches:

"I Jesus have sent my angel to you with this testimony for the churches. I am the root and the offspring of David, the bright morning star" (22:16). Matthew and Luke's genealogies report David is an ancestor of Jesus. And various New Testament writers pick up on this ancestry. In the throne room in Revelation 5:5, John learns the Lion of Judah, who turns out to be the Lamb who was slain, is the Root of David.

Invitation

Now comes an open invitation to drink the water of life – come to salvation:

The Spirit and the Bride say, "Come." And let him who hears say, "Come." And let him who is thirsty come, let him who desires take the water of life without price (22:17).

God's Spirit and all faithful Christians extend this invitation to come to the water. And everyone who hears the invitation is invited to tell others to come along also. Then the gate is thrown wide open for anyone who is thirsty to come to the water. Salvation is free to all comers.

This invitation reflects Jesus's invitation to the crowds at the

Feast of Tabernacles:

On the last day of the feast, the great day, Jesus stood up and proclaimed, "If any one thirst, let him come to me and drink. He who believes in me, as the scripture has said, 'Out of his heart shall flow rivers of living water'" (John 7:37-38).

Warnings

Then come final warnings:

I warn every one who hears the words of the prophecy of this book: if any one adds to them, God will add to him the plagues described in this book, and if any one takes away from the words of the book of this prophecy, God will take away his share in the tree of life and in the holy city, which are described in this book (22:18-19).

John writes a message from Christ, and, as he takes leave of his readers in the seven churches, he demands that they take his message to heart, act on it, and live by it. If they fail, they may be among those who receive the mark of the beast-emperor rather than those who bear the name of God on their foreheads (Revelation 7:3; 14:1).

A Closing Promise

One final time, Jesus, *who testifies to these things*, says, *"Surely I am coming soon."*

This is the last promise from Jesus in the next to last verse on the last page of the last book of the Christian Bible. As the centuries and nearly two millennia have rolled past, some have lost heart with no sign of Christ's return.

Edmund A. Steimle thought of this loss of hope as he noticed a statue of the Angel Gabriel atop New York City's Riverside Church. Dr. Steimle taught homiletics at New York's Union Theological Seminary just around the corner from Riverside. Gabriel traditionally is expected to blow his trumpet to herald the end of the age, and the statue perched on the church has his trumpet to his lips as if to sound the note of Christ's return. But Dr. Steimle commented on Gabriel and his horn in an Advent sermon, "The God of Hope" in his book, *Disturbed by Joy*:

Day by day he stands there at the ready. Warmed by summer sun, frozen by winter sleet, year after year goes by, but there is no mighty blast. Not even a tentative toot.[51]

But Dr. Steimle concluded his sermon by asserting the figure of Gabriel is really not ridiculous or irrelevant. Rather, the statue's frozen presence is "the constant reminder . . . that God's will of love will be done . . . Christ was not born in vain and those who give themselves to his life of love do not live in vain or die in vain."[52]

A Threefold Prayer

In response to Christ's thrice-stated promise to return soon, Revelation ends with a threefold prayer: *Amen. Come, Lord Jesus! The grace of the Lord Jesus Christ be with all the saints. Amen.*

Amen means "So be it" or "May it be so."

Come, Lord Jesus! says, in effect, "Yes, Lord, come on!"

Then, the final verse is a prayer for all God's people everywhere: *The grace of the Lord Jesus Christ be with all the saints. Amen.*

Whether Christ comes for you and me in some epochal event with the blast of a trumpet at the end of life on this planet or in our individual deaths, this is our great hope.

So we say, "Amen. May it be so."

Whispering Hope

Septimus Winner (1827-1902) wrote songs in a variety of genres, including "Oh Where, Oh Where Has My Little Dog Gone," "Listen to the Mocking Bird," and "Give Us Back Our Old Commander: Little Mac, the People's Pride," a plea to President Lincoln to return Union General George McClellan to service. The last-named song led to Winner's being court-martialed and jailed for treason, but he was released on his promise to destroy all remaining copies of the song.[53]

Soon after the Civil War ended (1868), Winner wrote the memorable hymn, "Whispering Hope," which seems to gather up themes from Revelation: The opening reference to "the voice of an angel" reminds us that much of Author John's hope comes from angel messages. References to darkness and dawn recall how the seven churches were facing times of darkness, as John points to brighter days after pressure from the emperor's enforcers of worship. The final stanza is directly based on Scripture, not from Revelation but from Hebrews 6:19-20:

We have this as a sure and steadfast anchor of the soul, a hope that enters into the inner shrine behind the curtain, where Jesus has gone as a forerunner on our behalf, having become a high priest for ever after the order of Melchizedek.

Soft as the voice of an angel,
Breathing a lesson unheard,
Hope with a gentle persuasion
Whispers her comforting word:
Wait till the darkness is over,
Wait till the tempest is done,
Hope for the sunshine tomorrow,
After the shower is gone.

If, in the dusk of the twilight,
Dim be the region afar,
Will not the deepening darkness
Brighten the glimmering star?
Then when the night is upon us,
Why should the heart sink away?
When the dark midnight is over,
Watch for the breaking of day.

Hope, as an anchor so steadfast,
Rends the dark veil for the soul,
Whither the Master has entered,
Robbing the grave of its goal.
Come then, O come, glad fruition,
Come to my sad weary heart;
Come, O Thou blest hope of glory,
Never, O never depart.

Whispering hope, Oh how welcome thy voice,
Making my heart in its sorrow rejoice.[54]

Appendix A: The Rapture

The main access to a camp for boys, high in the mountains, is a narrow two-lane road that turns back on itself time and again. During the week, youths swim, hike, do crafts, explore nature, and camp out one night. Because the camp is church-sponsored, the boys also have Bible study, a missionary speaker, and a nightly sermon in the chapel at the highest peak on the property.

With concern for the spiritual well-being of the campers, the pastor for the week gives an evangelistic sermon on Friday night, encouraging boys who have not made public professions of faith in Christ to take that stand before they start for home the next morning.

Pastors influenced by the Darby-Scofield school of thought have been known to warn the boys to think about the people who will drive them home: "Fellows, if you haven't accepted Jesus, what will happen if Jesus comes back while you are riding down that mountain? If your driver is saved, he will be taken away, and the car will have no one to guide it. You could go hurtling into the gorge and die and go to hell."

Variations on this Rapture theme are common in preaching to adults in church settings as well as with children and youth in camp.

At the end of this section we will examine verses in Revelation people of this mindset say refer to the Rapture. But be alert: Amy and Associates may be on hand.

The Rapture concept points to an event setting a series of end-time happenings in motion, including a seven-year Tribulation, the appearance of the Antichrist, the Battle of Armageddon, and the Millennium or thousand-year reign of Jesus on an earthly throne in Jerusalem.

As the scriptural basis for belief in the Rapture, 1 Thessalonians 4:13-18 is the foundational passage. Verses 16-17 are key verses and the words *caught up* in verse 17 are the particular focus:

For the Lord himself will descend from heaven with a cry of com-

mand, with the archangel's call, and with the sound of the trumpet of God. And the dead in Christ will rise first; then we who are alive, who are left, shall be caught up together with them in the clouds to meet the Lord in the air; and so we shall always be with the Lord.

Again, the words *caught up* are the emphasis for those who believe we are in the end times. They earnestly believe the Lord is coming back any day now. Those words, *caught up*, are what they call the Rapture. They look forward to being raptured, *caught up*, with Christ and being whisked away to heaven. According to the *Left Behind* books and movies, the raptured ones will leave their clothes and all their personal effects behind. If they are driving cars, the vehicles will go out of control, and God have pity on those who are left behind.

Certainly, you can build a case for the Rapture as they conceive it, based on that verse. But however you interpret that verse, we need to look at verses 13-15 just before this. When St. Paul writes his letters, he is addressing questions the people in the particular church are asking. The people in Thessalonica are concerned about the status of their loved ones, fellow Christians, who have died. They want to know what will happen to them. And the main point in this passage is to reassure the folks in this church that their loved ones will be okay. In fact, he says, Christ will bring the dead with Him, and all of them will go home to heaven:

[13] But we would not have you ignorant, brethren, concerning those who are asleep, that you may not grieve as others do who have no hope. [14] For since we believe that Jesus died and rose again, even so, through Jesus, God will bring with him those who have fallen asleep. [15] For this we declare to you by the word of the Lord, that we who are alive, who are left until the coming of the Lord, shall not precede those who have fallen asleep.

Then he goes on to describe how those who were dead and those who are alive will be caught up to be with the Lord always. And this is intended to bring reassurance. He concludes in verse 18 with another emphasis on reassurance: *Therefore comfort one another with these words.*

Many reputable scholars say the main point here is the destiny of the deceased Christians. If we put the main focus where Paul puts it, the specifics of how the saints unite with Christ is of secondary importance. But the futurists reverse those emphases.

End-time people also see the Rapture in Matthew 24.

Matthew devotes this chapter and the next to Jesus's eschatological teaching. The overriding theme in the two chapters is the need to be ready to give account for oneself when Christ returns and the repeated emphasis on the uncertainty of when that will occur. Rapturists focus particular attention on verses 40-42:

[40] Then two men will be in the field; one is taken and one is left. [41] Two women will be grinding at the mill; one is taken and one is left. [42] Watch therefore, for you do not know on what day your Lord is coming.

If we examine the larger context, we see these verses are followed immediately by three parables in chapter 25, all emphasizing separation of the faithful, the prepared, from the unfaithful and unprepared: ten young women who await the coming of the bridegroom (verses 1-13); three servants called to account for how they handled their master's money (verses 14-30); and two groups in the final judgment who are judged on whether they have shown compassion to the least of these (verses 40, 45).

The overall setting in Matthew 24-25, then, emphasizes separation of the godly from the ungodly.

Those who find the Rapture in the separation of the men in the field and the women at the mill need to account for the words from Jesus in 24:34:

Truly, I say to you, this generation will not pass away till all these things take place.

Rapturists tend to apply that statement to their own generation in the twenty-first century rather than to the first century when it was written. But they have to stretch the usual meaning of *genera-*

tion to find that meaning.

Rapture in Revelation? In preparing for accreditation re-evaluation, a committee of high school teachers was assigned to review a designated program in their school. In their initial meeting, they decided they wanted to come out with a 3.8 out of a possible 4.0 grade. Then they worked to make that their outcome, rather than looking objectively at the program and letting their research determine the grade. This approach to gathering information, known as confirmation bias, favors facts that support foregone conclusions. Some people study the Bible, determined to find support for their understanding of the Rapture. Their search includes the following passages:

Revelation 1:7 – *Behold, he is coming with the clouds, and every eye will see him, every one who pierced him; and all tribes of the earth will wail on account of him. Even so. Amen.*

For those who want to see the Rapture, they find it here. But there is nothing in this verse remotely suggesting people will be *caught up* to meet the Lord in the air. This seems to be confirmation bias.

Revelation 12:4-5 – *[4] And the dragon stood before the woman who was about to bear a child, that he might devour her child when she brought it forth; [5] she brought forth a male child, one who is to rule all the nations with a rod of iron, but her child was caught up to God and to his throne.*

Although the male child who will rule with a rod of iron is Christ, it seems a stretch to interpret His being taken to heaven as the Rapture. There is nothing here to show the child is accompanied by the saints of the centuries and those currently alive.

Rapture in the Old Testament? A Google search reveals far-fetched typology that even finds the Rapture in Old Testament:
- Enoch was translated or "caught up" to be with God : *Enoch*

walked with God; and he was not, for God took him (Genesis 5:24).
- Angels removed Abraham's nephew Lot and his family from Sodom to escape tribulation: *But he lingered; so the men seized him and his wife and his two daughters by the hand, the LORD being merciful to him, and they brought him forth and set him outside the city.* (Genesis 19:16). The rapturist emphasis here apparently is on Lot and his family being brought forth by the angels.
- Rahab, a harlot, protected Israelite spies who came to Jericho as they searched out their Promised Land. She was spared, along with her family, when the city was destroyed.

Then she let them down by a rope through the window, for her house was built into the city wall, so that she dwelt in the wall. And she said to them, "Go into the hills, lest the pursuers meet you; and hide yourselves there three days, until the pursuers have returned; then afterward you may go your way" (Joshua 2:15-16). Is the rapture seen here in the spies going on their way?

- The Song of Songs (or Song of Solomon) graphically describes physical love between a man and a woman, interpreted by some as representing Christ and the Church. In a great stretch to find the Rapture, the groom calls to his love, *Arise, my love, my fair one, and come away* (2:10). The rapturists apparently emphasize the woman being called to *arise . . . and come away.*

Seeing the Rapture in any or all these passages requires considerable effort and lively imagination.

Appendix B: The Great Tribulation

Parents often buy bicycles or toys for birthdays or Christmas and take them home, expecting simply to put them in the family room or under the tree, to be revealed on the Big Day. But then they discover the notice on the side of the box: "Some assembly required."

The concept of the Tribulation and the larger framework of Darby-Scofield eschatology are like those toys. The overall picture does not readily fit together without some careful assembling of the various parts.

Simply stated, the Tribulation is a seven-year period related to the Rapture. But this relationship really cannot be simply stated because futurists do not agree about the connection between the two events: There are pre-Tribulation rapturists, mid-Tribulation rapturists, and post-Tribulation rapturists.

Tribulation is a biblical term, but the Great Tribulation as envisioned by the futurists is a patchwork quilt approach to the Bible. Nowhere does the Bible say, clearly and directly, there will be a seven-year Tribulation at the end time, and nowhere does the Bible say, clearly and directly, there is a connection between the Rapture and the Tribulation. As indicated in Appendix A, affirmation of the Rapture in the Darby-Scofield system likewise requires some assembling of various Bible passages in order to make them fit together.

Strong's Exhaustive Concordance of the Bible,[55] for the faithful King James Version, on which futurists rely, lists twenty-six instances of *tribulation,* singular and plural.

All four of the Old Testament passages, singular and plural, refer to general trials and difficulties, rather than to end-time expectations (Deuteronomy 4:30; Judges 10:14; 1 Samuel 26:24; 1 Samuel 10:19).

Most New Testament usage, likewise, is absent any eschatological reference (Matthew 13:21; John 16:33; Acts 14:22; Romans 2:9;

Romans 5:3, plural and singular; Romans 8:35; Romans 12:12; 2 Corinthians 1:4; 2 Corinthians 7:4; 1 Thessalonians 3:4; 2 Thessalonians 1:6; Revelation 1:9; Revelation 2:9; Revelation 2:10; Revelation 2:22; Ephesians 3:13; 2 Thessalonians 1:4). Moreover, most of the New Testament passages are directed to Christians who are suffering or can expect to suffer tribulation; whereas the Darby-Scofield system generally depicts Christians being removed from the earth, with only those "left behind" suffering tribulation.

This leaves four New Testament verses that pertain to great periods of general tribulation:

Matthew 24:21 – *For then shall be great tribulation, such as was not since the beginning of the world to this time, no, nor ever shall be.*

Matthew 24:29 – *Immediately after the tribulation of those days shall the sun be darkened, and the moon shall not give her light, and the stars shall fall from heaven, and the powers of the heavens shall be shaken . . .*

Mark 13:24 – *But in those days, after that tribulation, the sun shall be darkened, and the moon shall not give her light.*

In these parallel passages, Jesus warns His listeners – presumably believers and non-believers alike – to flee when they see signs of the tribulation. Go as far away from Jerusalem as they possibly can, and pray this will not happen in winter when escape would be more difficult. Many scholars interpret these passages as referring to the destruction of Jerusalem rather than to the end time.

Regardless of which event is intended, we should not overlook Matthew 24:34 – *Truly, I say to you, this generation will not pass away till all these things take place.* This clearly is not intended for some later generation, even though some ignore the context and assume *this generation* pertains to the one in which they live. That, too, seems to require some assembly.

Finally, Revelation uses the word tribulation only in 7:13-14 – *Then one of the elders addressed me, saying, "Who are these, clothed in white robes, and whence have they come?" And I said unto him, Sir, thou knowest. And he said to me, These are they which came out of* great tribulation, and have washed their robes, and made them white in the blood of the Lamb.

The preceding verses indicate a vast host, beyond number, clearly believers, who have been through great tribulation. To interpret these martyrs as sinners "left behind" who converted during the tribulation, as envisioned by the futurists requires considerable assembly.

Other passages in Revelation do contain vivid descriptions of great peril falling on the unrighteous as judgment from God, although the term *tribulation* is not used. By inference, rapturists connect these descriptions to the total Darby-Scofield system of Rapture, Tribulation, Mark of the Beast, Armageddon, and Millennium. Here are examples:

With the opening of the sixth and next-to-the last seal, there is an earthquake, the sun and moon are darkened, stars fall to earth, the sky vanishes, and mountains and islands are removed from their places. All this causes earth's movers and shakers and ordinary people alike to plead for protection from the wrath of God and the Lamb (6:12-17).

In the lengthy passage when seven angels blow their trumpets (8:7-9:21), there is general chaos and destruction on land and sea, with hail, fire, darkness, and with stars falling from heaven. A veritable army of locusts torture those who do not have the seal of God on their foreheads. They are like no other locusts known to humanity:

In appearance the locusts were like horses arrayed for battle; on their heads were what looked like crowns of gold; their faces were like human faces, their hair like women's hair, and their teeth like lions' teeth; they had scales like iron breastplates, and the noise of their wings was like the noise of many chariots with horses rushing into battle. They have tails like scorpions, and stings, and their power of hurting men for five months lies in their tails (8:7-10).

In further symbolic language, the locusts are followed by two hundred million cavalrymen on unique horses (9:15-21):

[T]he riders wore breastplates the color of fire and of sapphire and of sulphur, and the heads of the horses were like lions' heads, and fire and smoke and sulphur issued from their mouths. By these three plagues a third of mankind was killed, by the fire and smoke and sulphur issuing from their mouths. For the power of the horses is in their mouths and in their tails; their tails are like serpents, with heads, and by means of them they wound. The rest of mankind, who were not killed by these plagues, did not repent of the works of their hands nor give up worshiping demons and idols of gold and silver and bronze and stone and wood, which cannot either see or hear or walk; nor did they repent of their murders or their sorceries or their immorality or their thefts.

In chapter 16:1-11, as seven angels pour out the bowls of God's wrath, further death and destruction rains down on earth, sea, fresh water, and the air.

All this is prelude to the fall of Babylon-Rome in chapters 17-18.

So a literal reading supports the idea of great destruction, leading up to a bloody battle at Armageddon. But, as we have noted in chapter 8 of this book, in keeping with symbolism throughout Revelation, the only weaponry at Armageddon is one lone sword – the word of Christ that issues from His mouth (1:16 and 19:15 and 21).

A great deal of the Tribulation concept is based in the Old Testament book of Daniel. Like most of Revelation, the latter half of Daniel is apocalyptic, using figurative language and cryptic numbers, in a setting marked by dark struggle between godly and evil forces.

Daniel 9:24-27 is a crucial passage for the futurist view of the Tribulation:

[24] Seventy weeks are determined upon thy people and upon thy holy city, to finish the transgression, and to make an end of sins, and to make reconciliation for iniquity, and to bring in everlasting righteousness, and to seal up the vision and prophecy, and to anoint the most Holy. [25] Know therefore and understand, that from the go-

ing forth of the commandment to restore and to build Jerusalem unto the Messiah the Prince shall be seven weeks, and threescore and two weeks: the street shall be built again, and the wall, even in troublous times. [26] And after threescore and two weeks shall Messiah be cut off, but not for himself: and the people of the prince that shall come shall destroy the city and the sanctuary; and the end thereof shall be with a flood and unto the end of the war desolations are determined. [27] And he shall confirm the covenant with many for one week: and in the midst of the week he shall cause the sacrifice and the oblation to cease, and for the overspreading of abominations he shall make it desolate, even until the consummation, and that determined shall be poured upon the desolate.

The seventy weeks in this passage generally were interpreted in non-canonical Jewish writings as seventy weeks of years or four hundred ninety years, with each day representing a year and, thus, each week representing seven years. In keeping with that understanding, futurists see the seven weeks in verse 25 as forty-nine years in rebuilding the Temple after the Exile. Then the sixty-two weeks or four hundred thirty-four years in verse 26 are the time between the Temple's restoration and the time Jesus was crucified: *And after threescore and two weeks shall Messiah be cut off. . .*

Seven weeks and sixty-two weeks total sixty-nine weeks, or four hundred eighty-three years, leaving one week or seven years to go. Then, futurists say, the clock stopped when the Jews rejected their Messiah, and it still is stopped. This is the Church Age, which will last until the Rapture when the Church will be taken out of the world. The clock then will resume ticking and the Tribulation will begin. It will run for that final week or seven years. The Antichrist will have full sway as he establishes the one-world government which presumably will prevail until the Battle of Armageddon.

In context, this passage seems to contain nothing that points to a delay of thousands of years between week sixty-nine and week seventy. This is another instance of "some assembly required" to fit the requirements of Darby-Scofield.

A guiding principle of interpretation throughout this present book is that all the biblical books were written to bring words of hope, encouragement, and — at times — chastening to the original readers. That has been our basic approach for understanding Revelation. With that principle in mind, we assume Daniel's primary message was for people who lived before the time of Jesus. There are different schools of thought as to when Daniel was written, depending on whether the apocalyptic sections are viewed as prophecy or history. Whatever its date, we have to ask, what hope would the book offer those readers in the pre-Christian era if its primary message were intended for people in some far distant era such as ours?

Bibliography

My earliest conscious effort to understand this often misunderstood New Testament book came when Dr. Ray Summers (then a professor at Southwestern Baptist Theological Seminary in Fort Worth) gave a series of lectures at the Glorieta Baptist Conference Center in Glorieta, New Mexico, in the early 1950s. Across the intervening six decades, my thinking has been shaped by other writers and lecturers, including those listed below.

Morris Ashcraft, "Revelation," *The Broadman Bible Commentary*, Volume 12 (Nashville: Broadman Press, 1972).

William Barclay, *The Revelation of John, Volume 2, The Daily Bible Study Series*, Revised Edition (Philadelphia: The Westminster Press, 1976).

James L. Blevins, *Revelation as Drama* (Nashville: Broadman Press, 1984).

John Wick Bowman, *The Drama of the Book of Revelation* (Philadelphia; Westminster Press, 1955).

Craig R. Koester, A Video: *Apocalypse: Controversies and Meaning in Western History* (Chantilly, Virginia: The Teaching Company, 2011).

Charles M. Laymon, *The Book of Revelation (*New York and Nashville: Abingdon Press, 1960).

Edward A. McDowell, *The Meaning and Message of the Book of Revelation (*Nashville: Broadman Press, 1951).

Bruce M. Metzger, *Breaking the Code, Understanding the Book of Revelation* (Nashville: Abingdon Press, 1993).

Barbara R. Rossing, The Rapture Exposed, The Message of Hope in the Book of Revelation (Cambridge, Massachusetts: Westview Press, 2004).

Justin A. Smith, *Commentary on the Revelation, An American Commentary on the New Testament,* Volume VII (Philadelphia: American Baptist Publication Society, 1884).

Ray Summers, *Worthy is the Lamb*: *Interpreting the Book of Revelation in Its Historical Context* (Nashville: Broadman Press, 1951).

Notes

Chapter 1

1 Fanny J. Crosby, "Safe in the Arms of Jesus," *The Broadman Hymnal* (Nashville: Broadman Press, 1940), Hymn 353.

Chapter 2

2 Walter Brueggemann, *The Prophetic Imagination* ((Minneapolis: Fortress Press, 1978), pp. 13f.

3 *Ibid.*, p. 13.

4 *Ibid.*, p. 15.

5 George Duffield, "Stand Up, Stand Up for Jesus," *The Broadman Hymnal* (Nashville: Broadman Press, 1940), Hymn 31.

Chapter 3

6 Francis of Assisi, "All Creatures of Our God and King" (http://www.cyberhymnal.org/htm/a/c/acoogak.htm).

7 Bill Staines, "All God's Creatures Have a Place in the Choir." (*BusSongs.com*. http://bussongs.com/songs/gods-creatures-place-choir.php).

8 Joseph Swain, "O Thou in Whose Presence," *The Methodist Hymnal* (Nashville: The Methodist Publishing House, 1964, 1966), Hymn 129.

Chapter 4

9 John Wick Bowman, *The Drama of the Book of Revelation* (Philadelphia; Westminster Press, 1955).

10 James L. Blevins, *Revelation as Drama* (Nashville: Broadman Press, 1984).

11 Joe Masteroff, John Kander, and Fred Ebb, *Cabaret*. (New York, Toronto et al: Scholastic Book Service, 1967).

12 I read this interview with Signe Hasso in *The Atlanta Constitution*

in April 1969 before I saw the show. I no longer have the clipping of he story.

13 Grantland Rice, "The Four Horsemen," *New York Herald Tribune* (New York: New York Herald Tribune, October 18, 1924).

14 Tim Wolfe, Sculptor, *Notre Dame Four Horsemen Sculpture* (AllSculptures.com http://www.allsculptures.com/proddetail.php?prod=Notre+Dame+Four+Horsemen+Sculpture&gclid=COv54Ifyu78CFWQQ7AodfD8AoQ#.U78guVZ38aU.

14-A Ray Summers, *Worth is the Lamb* (Nashville: Broadman Press, 1951), p. 159.

14-B Justin A. Smith, "Commentary on the Revelation," *An American Commentary on the New Testament*, Volume VII (Philadelphia: American Baptist Publication Society, 1884), p. 142.

15 Edward Mote, "The Solid Rock," *The Broadman Hymnal* (Nashville: Broadman Press, 1940), Hymn 96.

Chapter 5

16 Dawson McAllister with Clark Albright, *Pack Your Bags – Jesus Is Coming* (Irving, Texas: Shepherd Ministries, 1993), p. 49.

17 "US town escapes 666 phone prefix" (textually.org http://www.textually.org/textually/archives/2008/01/018537.htm, January 3, 2008).

17a Associated Press, "Bible college gets 666 phone prefix," *(DiscussAnything.com* http://www.discussanything.com/forums/showthread.php/23741-Bible-college-gets-666-phon, January 18, 2003).

18 Information on John Nelson Darby and C. I. Scofield can readily be found online. Darby: "John Nelson Darby, Father of Dispensationalism," *ChristianHistory.net* (http://www.christianitytoday.com/ch/131christians/pastorsandpreachers/darby.html?start=1); Larry V. Crutchfield, "John Nelson Darby: Defender of the Faith," *According to Prophecy Ministries Present's [sic] Pre-Trib Perspectives Articles Directory* (http://www.according2prophecy.org/darby.html); "John Nelson Darby," *Theopedia* (http://www.theopedia.com/John_Nelson_Darby).
Scofield: Daniel Scofield, "Biography - Dr. C. I. Scofield," *BibleSanity.org*

(http://biblesanity.org/scofield.htm); Texe Marrs, "The Shocking Truth About C. I. Scofield," *Jesus-is-Savior.com* (http://www.jesus-is-savior.com/Wolves/scofield.htm).
The entire Scofield edition of the King James Bible is available online: "Scofield Reference Notes (1917 Edition)," *BibleStudyTools.com* (http://www.biblestudytools.com/commentaries/scofield-reference-notes/).

19 Martin Luther, "A Mighty Fortress," *The Broadman Hymnal* (Nashville: Broadman Press, 1940), Hymn 38.

20 Luther, "Ein' feste Burg ist unser Gott," *The Lutheran Hymnal* (Minneapolis: Fortress Press), Hymn 262.

21 Fr. Seraphim Rose, "The Twelve Signs of the End of the World," (http://orthodoxengland.org.uk/1982).

22 David J. Stewart, "Why the Antichrist Must Come Soon," *Jesus-is-Savior.com* ((Stewart http://www.jesus-is-savior.com/End%20of%20the%20World/antichrist_must_come_soon.htm).

23 "The Antichrist," Catholic Answers (http://www.catholic.com/tracts/the-antichrist).

24 Richard Kyle, *The Last Days Are Here Again, A History of the End Times*. (Grand Rapids, Mich.: Baker Books, 1998), p. 51.

25 *Ibid.*, p. 47.

26 Ibid.

27 *Ibid.* p. 68.

28 Merrill C. Tenney, *Interpreting Revelation* (Grand Rapids, Michigan: Wm. B. Eerdmans Publishing Company, 1957) p. 197.

29 Kendell Easley, *Living with the End in Sight* (Nashville, Tennessee: Holman Bible Publishers, 2000) p. 57.

Chapter 6

30 Julia Ward Howe, "Mine Eyes Have Seen the Glory of the Coming of the Lord," *WWW.Chess.com* (http://www.chess.com/groups/forumview/

mine-eyes-have-seen-the-glory-of-the-coming-of-the-lord5).

31 Jone Johnson Lewis, "Battle Hymn of the Republic - History and Words," *about.com women's history*. (http://womenshistory.about.com/library/etext/bl_howe_battle_hymn.htm).

32 "Julia Ward Howe," *Infoplease* (http://www.infoplease.com/biography/var/juliawardhowe.html).

33 Charles Wesley, "Rejoice, the Lord is King," Cyber Hymnal (http://cyberhymnal.org/htm/r/e/rejtlord.htm).

Chapter 7

34 Percy Bysshe Shelley, "Ozymandias," *The Literature of England, Third Single Volume Edition*, eds. George K. Anderson, William E. Buckler, Mary Harris Veeder. (Glenvew, Illinois et al: Scott, Foresman and Company, 1953, 1967, 1979) p. 759.

35 *Ibid*.

36 "Robert Green Lee (1886-1978)," *Theology thru Technology, tlogical* (http://www.tlogical.net/biorglee.htm).

37 William Cowper, "God Moves in a Mysterious Way," *Timeless Truths, Free Online Library* (http://library.timelesstruths.org/music/God_Moves_in_a_Mysterious_Way).

Chapter 8

38 Thornton Wilder, *Our Town*. (*Quotes.net*. STANDS4 LLC, 2014. Web. 11 Jul 2014. <http://www.quotes.net/mquote/70976>.)

39 Ernest W. Shurtleff, "Lead On, O King Eternal," *The Methodist Hymnal* (Nashville: The Methodist Publishing House, 1964, 1966), Hymn 478.

Chapter 9

40 Video of Rudy Vallee singing "My Time is Your Time," *Who's Dating Who?* (http://music.whosdatedwho.com/tpx_22629232/my-time-is-your-time/).

41 "Rudy Vallee, 30's Singling Idol and 'Vagabond Lover,' Dead, *The New York Times*, July 4, 1986.

42 Isaac Watts, "Jesus Shall Reign Where'er the Sun," The Lutheran Hymnal (http://www.lutheran-hymnal.com/lyrics/tlh511.htm).

43 Jonathan Edwards, "Sinners in the Hands of an Angry God," *Christian Classics Ethereal Library* (http://www.ccel.org/ccel/edwards/sermons.sinners.html).

44 Will L. Thompson, "There's a Great Day Coming," *The Broadman Hymnal* (Nashville: Broadman Press, 1940), Hymn 333.

45 _____, "Softly and Tenderly," *The Broadman Hymnal* (Nashville: Broadman Press, 1940), Hymn 100.

Chapter 10

46 John Keats, "Endymion," *The Literature of England, Third Single Volume Edition*, eds. George K. Anderson, William E. Buckler, Mary Harris Veeder. (Glenvew, Illinois et al: Scott, Foresman and Company, 1953, 1967, 1979) p. 776.

47 Arthur F. Ingler, "The Pearly White City," *Hymns Unto God* (http://www.hymnsuntogod.org/Hymns-PD/T-Hymns/The-Pearly-White-City.html).

48 James L. Blevins, *Revelation as Drama* (Nashville: Broadman Press, 1984), pp. 7-10.

49 *Ibid.*, pp. 147-191.

50 *Ibid.*, pp. 190f.

51 Edmund A. Steimle, *Disturbed by Joy*. (Philadelphia: Fortress Press, 1967), p. 14.

52 *Ibid.*, p. 22.

53 Sarah Winnemucca, "Septimus Winner," American National Biography Online (http://www.anb.org/articles/18/18-03837.html).

54 Septimus Winner, "Whispering Hope," The Broadman Hymnal (Nashville: Broadman Press, 1940), Hymn 466.

Appendix B

55 James Strong, *Strong's Exhaustive Concordance* (Nashville: Crusade Bible Publishers, Inc.), No Date Included.